THE STORY OF
THE BIBLE

VOLUME II
THE NEW TESTAMENT

TEST BOOK
WITH ANSWER KEY

CONTENTS

And the Word became flesh and dwelt among us,
full of grace and truth; we have beheld his glory,
glory as of the only Son from the Father.

— John 1:14

THE NEW TESTAMENT

A Word to the Teacher

More than eighty years have passed since the publication of *Bible History: A Textbook of the Old and New Testaments for Catholic Schools* (1931). The book soon became a standard text in Catholic schools, for students in the grades we would now call middle school. Since that time, *Bible History* has become a popular text for Catholic homeschooled students.

The time has now come for an updated version that is more complete and more accessible to contemporary readers. The new and expanded version of the textbook, published by TAN Books as *The Story of the Bible*, appears in two volumes: Volume 1, *The Old Testament*, and Volume 2, *The New Testament*. Vocabulary, style, and historical and geographical references have been updated; the text features a new design with fresh illustrations; and some of the material has been reorganized for a clearer presentation.

Most significantly, the New Testament history, which previously focused on the Gospels and concluded with the events reported in Acts 2, now includes six additional chapters. These final chapters tell about the last decades of the biblical story as the newborn Church grew rapidly and began to suffer persecution. They take readers through the remainder of the Book of Acts, focusing—as that book does—on the ministries of the Apostles Peter and Paul. The last chapter concludes with brief remarks about how the New Testament epistles and the Book of Revelation, though not themselves historical narratives, nevertheless contribute to our historical knowledge of the earliest Christians.

Enhanced Storytelling

The new title, *The Story of the Bible*, reflects a new emphasis in presentation on the narrative aspect of the biblical text. Young people love a good story, and the Scripture is full of good stories: in the Old Testament, from the poetic description of creation to the high dramas of prophets, kings, and conquerors; in the New Testament, from the compelling parables of Our Lord to the startling visions of the Apocalypse.

The storytelling aspect of the two new volumes has been especially enhanced in two ways. First, the dynamic style of the new illustrations contributes powerfully to the narrative. Second, an audio recording of the texts is now available so that students can enjoy the biblical stories, not just as readers, but also as listeners. The recording also makes it possible for younger students to enjoy the texts before they have acquired the reading vocabulary required for the books.

Using the Test Book

The revisions of the textbook were extensive enough to require a completely new test book. Like the previous test book, this one provides questions for each chapter that are suitable as a study exercise or as an objective answer test, with an answer key at the end. But the questions now include not only matching items, but multiple choice items as well (along with a few true/false), rather than fill-in-the-blank. Questions for Volume 2 of the textbook are included in this new test book.

Teachers should note that when Scripture is quoted in *The Story of the Bible*, quotations from the New Testament are now freely adapted from the *New Testament, Confraternity Text*. For this reason, the spelling of the names of people and places will reflect more contemporary usage, rather than the spellings in the older Douay-Rheims translation.

Finally, we should note that supplementary materials for use with the textbook and this test book are available for free download at the publisher's website: www.TANBooks.com.

St. Jerome, an ancient Doctor of the Church and Bible translator known as "the father of biblical scholarship," once said: "Ignorance of Scripture is ignorance of Christ." Our prayer is that *The Story of the Bible* and the accompanying test books will tell the story of Scripture in such a way that young readers will be drawn closer to Our Lord, who is Himself the eternal Word of God.

The Editors

INTRODUCTION
Your Time Has Come

Textbook pages: 7–12
Perfect score: 100

Your Score: _____

Multiple Choice

Directions: For each numbered item, circle the letter beside the choice (A, B, C, or D) that best answers the question or completes the statement. Circle only one choice per item. Each correct answer is worth 4 points. 60 possible points.

1. We can learn about God from:

A. the natural beauty and power of the things He has created.
B. the love of the people who care for us.
C. the Bible.
D. all of the above.

2. Which of the following does *not* demonstrate why the "Book of Nature" only partially teaches us all we need to know about God?

A. Sometimes we read the wonderful lessons found in the "Book of Nature" incorrectly.
B. The things of this world are so beautiful and powerful and good that we may be tempted to think more of them than we do of the God who made them.
C. The "Book of Nature" cannot be understood even in a limited way.
D. Many important things about God and His will for us are above and beyond nature.

3. A truth that is above and beyond nature is called:

A. natural.
B. preternatural.
C. unnatural.
D. supernatural.

4. The truths that we can't fully understand, even after God has told them to us, we call:

A. mysteries.
B. fables.
C. half-truths.
D. myths.

5. God gave the sacred writers who wrote the Bible a special kind of help that He has given to no other writers; we call this unique kind of assistance:

A. literary elegance.
B. clarity of speech.
C. divine inspiration.
D. natural law.

6. The Church cannot make a mistake when she tells us what we must believe and do if we wish to know, love, and serve God, both in this life and the next. In these matters, the Church is:

A. fallible.
B. infallible.
C. generally reliable.
D. uncertain.

7. The Bible is divided into two parts:

A. the Law and the Prophets.
B. the Old Testament and the New Testament.
C. the Gospel and the Epistles.
D. the Psalms and the Chronicles.

8. In the Bible, the word "testament" means:

A. a contract.
B. a commercial transaction.
C. a story.
D. a covenant.

9. The Old Testament tells us about:

A. the life of Jesus and His mother.
B. the history of the early Church in Jerusalem.
C. the history of all the nations in ancient times.
D. the covenant between God and His people before Jesus came into the world.

10. The New Testament tells us about:

A. how God's promise was fulfilled in Jesus Christ and His Church.
B. the history of the ancient Israelites.
C. the history of the Church in the Middle Ages.
D. the history of all the nations in modern times.

11. The primary purpose of the moral books in the Old Testament is to:

A. provide historical information about past events.
B. offer rules of conduct for how to live properly.
C. foretell things that will happen in the future.
D. entertain with interesting stories.

12. Another name for the Bible is:

A. Sacred Liturgy.
B. Sacred Scripture.
C. Lectio Divina.
D. Sacred Tradition.

13. Truths about our faith that were not written down in the Bible, but have come to us by word of mouth and by example, beginning with the apostles, are known as:

A. Sacred Liturgy.
B. Sacred Scripture.
C. Lectio Divina.
D. Sacred Tradition.

14. How many books does the Old Testament contain?

A. 29
B. 58
C. 46
D. 66

15. How many books does the New Testament contain?

A. 27
B. 58
C. 45
D. 66

Old Testament or New?

Directions: The following books are from the Bible. Write "OT" in the blank beside the name of a book if it appears in the Old Testament; write "NT" in the blank beside the name of a book if it appears in the New Testament. Note that the books of the Bible are usually called by the main word in their title. For example, *The Gospel According to St. Luke* is called *Luke*. Each blank is worth 2 points. 40 possible points.

1. _____ Revelation

2. _____ Romans

3. _____ Deuteronomy

4. _____ Matthew

5. _____ Sirach

6. _____ Luke

7. _____ Isaiah

8. _____ Jeremiah

9. _____ 1 and 2 Maccabees

10. _____ Genesis

11. _____ Daniel

12. _____ Psalms

13. _____ John

14. _____ Jude

15. _____ 1 and 2 Corinthians

16. _____ Judith

17. _____ Exodus

18. _____ Acts of the Apostles

19. _____ Leviticus

20. _____ Zechariah

PART ONE
How Christ Prepared to Redeem the World

CHAPTER 1
The World Into Which the Messiah Came

Textbook pages: 13–26
Perfect score: 100

Your Score: _____

Matching

Directions: In each blank beside a phrase, write the letter of the term that is described by that phrase. Each item is worth 2 points. 10 possible points.

A. Gabbatha
B. Herod's Temple
C. Antonia
D. procurator
E. Pinnacle

_____ 1. high tower on the southeast corner of the Temple

_____ 2. fortified building northwest of the Temple in Jerusalem where Roman soldiers were garrisoned

_____ 3. a large square or court where the procurator met the people on certain occasions

_____ 4. the Roman governor of Palestine

_____ 5. rebuilt after it had been partially destroyed by fire during a siege of Jerusalem

Matching: Cities and Provinces of Ancient Palestine

Directions: In each blank beside a phrase, write the letter of the term that is described by that phrase. Each item is worth 2 points. 14 possible points.

A. Galilee
B. Capernaum, Tiberias, Chorazin, Cana, Nazareth
C. Shechem, Sebaste, Caesarea

question continued on next page ➡

D. Jerusalem, Bethlehem, Jericho, Arimathea
E. Judea
F. Perea
G. Samaria

_____ 1. the principal cities of Judea

_____ 2. the central province of ancient Palestine

_____ 3. the major cities of Samaria

_____ 4. the northernmost province of ancient Palestine

_____ 5. the principal towns of Galilee

_____ 6. the southernmost province of ancient Palestine

_____ 7. the country on the far side of the Jordan, to the southeast

Matching: Coins of Ancient Palestine

Directions: In each blank beside a phrase, write the letter of the term that is described by that phrase. Each item is worth 2 points. 12 possible points.

A. denarius
B. drachma
C. stater
D. talent
E. didrachma
F. shekel

_____ 1. Greek coin equal to the denarius

_____ 2. Greek coin equal to two drachmas

_____ 3. Greek coin equal to a shekel

_____ 4. Greek coin worth more than fifteen years' wages for a laborer

_____ 5. Jewish coin equal to four denarii

_____ 6. Roman coin equal to a day's wage for a common laborer

Matching: Religious Life in Ancient Palestine

Directions: In each blank beside a phrase, write the letter of the term that is described by that phrase. Each item is worth 2 points. 24 possible points.

A. Nazarites
B. Sadducees
C. Sanhedrin
D. Essenes
E. Pharisees
F. scribes

G. Feast of Purim
H. chief priests
I. elders
J. high priest
K. Feast of the Dedication
L. phylacteries

_____ 1. presided over the Sanhedrin

_____ 2. ancient Jewish religious party whose purpose was to preserve the Sacred Scriptures and to keep them free from error

_____ 3. bands of parchment containing sacred texts

_____ 4. specialists in Jewish religious law

_____ 5. a class of men who took a vow to serve God by a life of penance and mortification

_____ 6. former high priests

_____ 7. ancient Jewish religious party who denied some of the newer teachings found in the Jewish Scriptures

_____ 8. Jewish ruling council of seventy-one members

_____ 9. the leading men of the Jewish people

_____ 10. ancient Jewish religious sect that lived apart from the people in communities governed by strict rules

_____ 11. known today as Hanukkah

_____ 12. commemorates the day when Queen Esther saved her people in Persia

Multiple Choice

Directions: For each numbered item, circle the letter beside the choice (A, B, C, or D) that best answers the question or completes the statement. Circle only one choice per item. Each correct answer is worth 4 points. 40 possible points.

1. Why did so many of the Jewish people of Jesus' time resent Herod the Great?

   A. Herod laid a great burden of taxes on the people.
   B. Herod refused to worship at the Temple.
   C. Herod was guilty of great cruelty, and he wasn't a Jew.
   D. Herod was extremely wealthy, but he did nothing to help the poor.

2. Why were the tax collectors so despised by the Jewish people?

   A. Tax collectors oppressed the people and took a portion of the taxes for themselves.
   B. Tax collectors were a constant reminder that the Jews were under the domination of a foreign power.
   C. Tax collectors who were themselves Jews were considered traitors to their nation.
   D. All of the above.

3. Why were there moneychangers in the Temple?

   A. To avoid extra weight, travelers carried with them only one or two coins of great value, so they needed to exchange these for multiple coins of lesser value.
   B. Only gold could be used to pay for Temple sacrifices, so the moneychangers exchanged gold for coins of other metals.
   C. Only Jewish money could be used to pay for Temple sacrifices, so the moneychangers exchanged Jewish coins for Greek and Roman coins.
   D. All of the above.

4. How did the Jewish people of Jesus' time usually eat their meals together?

   A. They reclined on cushions on the floor around dishes of food set in the middle, much like spokes around the hub of a wheel.
   B. They sat down in chairs around tables the same way we do today.
   C. They took their meals outside their homes and ate while sitting on the grass.
   D. They ate on the roof of the house, which served as an outside deck.

5. For the Jews, a day lasted:

   A. from midnight to midnight.
   B. from noon to noon.
   C. from sunset to sunset.
   D. from sunrise to sunset.

6. In the common way of reckoning time in Jesus' day, the "ninth hour" was:

A. 3 P.M.
B. 6 P.M.
C. 3 A.M.
D. noon.

7. In the time of Christ, which four languages were most commonly used in Palestine?

A. Hebrew, Aramaic, Persian, and Latin
B. Latin, Hebrew, Aramaic, and Egyptian
C. Greek, Latin, Aramaic, and Egyptian
D. Hebrew, Aramaic, Greek, and Latin

8. The Jewish festival that celebrates the rededication of the altar and the Temple by Judas Maccabeus is:

A. the Feast of Purim.
B. the Feast of the Dedication.
C. the Feast of Tabernacles.
D. the Feast of the Pasch.

9. How did the religion of the Samaritans differ from that of the rest of the Jews?

A. Their Bible consisted only of the first five books of our Bible.
B. They had their own temple on Mount Gerizim, which they insisted was the only temple of the true God.
C. Both A and B above.
D. None of the above.

10. The courts surrounding the Temple included:

A. the Court of the Priests, the Court of the Israelites, the Court of the Women, and the Court of the Gentiles.
B. the Court of the Priests, the Court of the Levites, the Court of the Pharisees, and the Court of the Gentiles.
C. the Court of the Levites, the Court of the Israelites, the Court of the Women, and the Court of the Gentiles.
D. the Court of the Priests, the Court of the Israelites, the Court of the Sadducees, and the Court of the Gentiles.

CHAPTER 2
The Redeemer Comes to Earth

Textbook pages: 27–40
Perfect score: 100

Your Score: _____

Matching

Directions: In each blank beside a phrase, write the letter of the term that is described by that phrase. You may match more than one description to a single term. Each item is worth 3 points. 45 possible points.

A. Zechariah
B. Nazareth
C. the *Benedictus*
D. Gabriel
E. Emmanuel
F. the *Magnificat*
G. Elizabeth
H. Egypt

I. Galilee
J. Augustus
K. Jesus
L. Simeon
M. the *Nunc Dimittis*
N. magi
O. Bethlehem

_____ 1. mother of John the Baptist

_____ 2. the messenger angel sent to Zechariah and to the Blessed Virgin Mother

_____ 3. Mary's prayer of praise and thanksgiving to the Lord for making her the mother of Jesus

_____ 4. father of John the Baptist

_____ 5. prophesied in the Temple about Jesus and Mary

_____ 6. Mary's hometown

_____ 7. the Roman emperor when Jesus was born

_____ 8. means "God with us"

_____ 9. Zechariah's prophecy about Jesus and John the Baptist

_____ 10. the town where Jesus was born

question continued on next page ➡

_____ 11. the province where Jesus spent most of His childhood

_____ 12. wise men from the East

_____ 13. Simeon's prophecy, spoken as he held the infant Jesus in his arms

_____ 14. means "Savior"

_____ 15. where Mary and Joseph took the infant Jesus to save His life

Multiple Choice

Directions: For each numbered item, circle the letter beside the choice (A, B, C, or D) that best answers the question or completes the statement. Circle only one choice per item. Each correct answer is worth 5 points. 55 possible points.

1. Why did Zechariah doubt the word of the angel?

A. Zechariah thought he was just hallucinating.
B. Zechariah thought the angel was a demon in disguise.
C. Zechariah thought that he and his wife were too old to have children.
D. In his heart, Zechariah really didn't want to have a child.

2. How did Mary respond when the angel told her that God wanted her to be the mother of His Son?

A. Mary said, "Let it be done to me according to your word."
B. Mary asked for more time to consider the proposal.
C. Mary said she needed to speak with Joseph before she agreed.
D. Mary expressed her concerns about being able to raise the child properly.

3. When Mary arrived at Elizabeth's home, how did Elizabeth know that Mary had been chosen to be Jesus' mother?

A. The news had traveled fast from Galilee to Judea.
B. Gabriel had visited Elizabeth as well to tell her the good news.
C. When Elizabeth saw Mary coming, she guessed the reason for the visit.
D. The Holy Spirit had revealed it to her.

4. What mission for John the Baptist was prophesied by his father?

A. John would be the Messiah that God had promised the Jewish people.
B. John would prepare the way of the Lord, giving people knowledge of salvation through the forgiveness of their sins.
C. John would raise an army to drive the Romans out of Palestine.
D. John would become the high priest in the Temple to make sacrifices for the sins of the people.

5. Why wasn't Jesus born in Nazareth, where Mary and Joseph lived?

A. Mary and Joseph were visiting Elizabeth in Judea when Jesus was born.
B. Mary and Joseph had just recently moved to another town.
C. Mary and Joseph had to travel to another town to enroll in the Roman emperor's census of the empire.
D. All of the above.

6. The opening words of the *Gloria* in the Mass, "Glory to God in the highest," come from what source?

A. These words were spoken by the angels to the shepherds on the night Jesus was born.
B. These words were written above the doors of the Temple in Jerusalem.
C. These words were prophesied by Zechariah when John the Baptist was born.
D. These words were part of Mary's song when she visited Elizabeth.

7. How do we know that Mary and Joseph were not wealthy?

A. If they were wealthy, they would not have been required to pay taxes to the Romans.
B. Joseph and Mary did not come from wealthy families.
C. When they presented Jesus in the Temple, they offered the sacrifice that the Law required of the poor.
D. If they were wealthy, they could have stayed in the inn instead of the stable.

8. What three gifts did the wise men bring to Jesus?

A. gold, silver, and myrrh
B. gold, pearls, and rubies
C. gold, jewels, and frankincense
D. gold, frankincense, and myrrh

9. Why did Herod ask the wise men where they found the Baby they were seeking?

A. He wanted to worship the Baby as well.
B. He wanted to kill the Baby so that the Child wouldn't become a rival to Herod's throne.
C. He wanted to bring kingly gifts to the Baby.
D. He wanted to adopt the Baby as his son and heir to the throne.

10. Why didn't Mary and Joseph ensure that Jesus was with them when they left Jerusalem after celebrating the Passover?

A. Since He was twelve years old, they considered Him old enough to take care of Himself.
B. They were having so much fun with relatives and friends that they forgot all about Jesus.
C. They probably thought Jesus was traveling home with one of His cousin's families.
D. An angel told Joseph in a dream to leave Jesus in Jerusalem so He could teach the people in the Temple.

11. The word that means "anointed by God" is:

A. Messiah.
B. Christ.
C. Both A and B above.
D. None of the above.

PART TWO
How Christ Ministered

CHAPTER 3
Christ Begins His Public Ministry

Textbook pages: 41–50
Perfect score: 100

Your Score: _____

Matching

Directions: In each blank beside a phrase, write the letter of the term that is described by that phrase. Each item is worth 2 points. 16 possible points.

A. disciples
B. Rabbi
C. Gospel
D. John the Baptist
E. Satan
F. apostles
G. Herod Antipas
H. Salome

_____ 1. lived in the desert, eating locusts and wild honey

_____ 2. means "teacher"

_____ 3. the ruler of Galilee and Perea

_____ 4. the good news about salvation

_____ 5. the Twelve who had a special mission in establishing Christ's Church

_____ 6. followers

_____ 7. performed a dance that led to death

_____ 8. tempted Jesus in the wilderness

Matching: The Apostles

Directions: In each blank beside a phrase, write the letter of the term that is described by that phrase. You may match more than one description to a single term. Each item is worth 2 points. 24 possible points.

A. Andrew
B. Cephas
C. Bartholomew
D. James and John
E. Peter
F. Simon
G. Matthew
H. Judas
I. James
J. Thaddeus
K. Philip
L. Thomas

_____ 1. Aramaic word for "rock"

_____ 2. the sons of Zebedee

_____ 3. the tax collector

_____ 4. also called Jude

_____ 5. the son of Alpheus

_____ 6. the name Jesus gave the fisherman known as Simon

_____ 7. told Nathanael that he had found the Messiah

_____ 8. Peter's brother

_____ 9. his name means "the Twin"

_____ 10. called the Zealot

_____ 11. came from Kerioth, a town in Judea

_____ 12. known also as Nathanael

Multiple Choice

Directions: For each numbered item, circle the letter beside the choice (A, B, C, or D) that best answers the question or completes the statement. Circle only one choice per item. Each correct answer is worth 6 points. 60 possible points.

1. Which Old Testament prophet had foretold the ministry of John the Baptist, calling him "a voice of one crying in the desert"?

A. Ezekiel
B. Elijah
C. Jeremiah
D. Isaiah

2. Which of the following was *not* accomplished by the baptism that John gave to people?

A. It was a sign of their repentance.
B. It washed away their sins.
C. It prepared their hearts for the coming of the Savior.
D. It demonstrated their intention to live a better life.

3. Why was John the Baptist reluctant to baptize Jesus?

A. John believed that Jesus should be baptizing him instead.
B. John feared that if He baptized Jesus, the people would leave John to follow Jesus.
C. John worried about what the Pharisees and Sadducees might say.
D. John didn't usually baptize his relatives.

4. What happened after John baptized Jesus?

A. The waters of the Jordan River parted, just as they had when Joshua's army marched through.
B. The Holy Spirit descended on Him in the form of a dove, and God the Father spoke from heaven.
C. The people watching all repented and began to follow Jesus.
D. A light from heaven shone down on John, and a voice cried out that his mission was completed.

5. Why did Jesus hide Himself away in the desert for forty days?

A. The Pharisees and Sadducees were asking Jesus too many questions.
B. Herod was still trying to find Jesus and kill Him.
C. Jesus was praying and fasting in preparation for the great work that lay ahead.
D. Jesus was weary from having so many people come to Him to be healed.

6. How did Jesus respond to the Devil's temptations in the desert?

A. Jesus quoted Scripture to show that the Devil's suggestions were against God's will.
B. Jesus stopped up His ears and refused to listen to the Devil.
C. Jesus debated the Devil with many arguments to show why the Devil was wrong.
D. Jesus told the Devil to come back later.

7. When Jesus sent the apostles out to preach and work miracles from city to city, why did He send them without money, food, or extra clothing?

A. Jesus simply didn't have enough money to provide these things for the apostles.
B. Jesus was testing the apostles to see how creative they could be in providing these things for themselves.
C. Jesus wanted them to depend on the faith and generosity of the people to whom they preached the gospel.
D. Jesus was testing God to see whether they could trust Him to provide these things.

8. What did Jesus tell His disciples was the main reason they should be joyful?

A. They should be joyful because their names were written in heaven.
B. They should be joyful because the demons obeyed them in Jesus' name.
C. They should be joyful because they could work miracles.
D. They should be joyful because all the people would love and honor them for their ministry.

9. Why did Herod Antipas order that John the Baptist be thrown into prison?

A. John had rebuked Herod publicly for committing a grave sin.
B. Herod feared that John would start a rebellion to overthrow him.
C. John had become quite wealthy, and Herod wanted to steal John's treasure.
D. Herod knew that if he threw John in prison, Jesus would come to visit John, and Herod could imprison Jesus as well.

10. How did John the Baptist die?

A. He came down with a fatal illness in prison.
B. He was attacked by wild beasts out in the desert.
C. He was betrayed and killed by one of his own disciples.
D. He was beheaded at Herod's command.

CHAPTER 4
Christ Calls All People to Repentance

Textbook pages: 51–66
Perfect score: 100

Your Score: _____

Matching

Directions: In each blank beside a phrase, write the letter of the term that is described by that phrase. You may match more than one description to a single term. Each item is worth 4 points. 40 possible points.

A. the Son of Man
B. Nicodemus
C. Mary Magdalene
D. Mary of Bethany
E. Martha
F. Simon
G. Zacchaeus
H. Sychar
I. Bethany

_____ 1. was delivered by Jesus from seven demons who had tormented her

_____ 2. sister of Lazarus who sat at Jesus' feet to listen

_____ 3. came under the cover of darkness to see Jesus

_____ 4. a Pharisee who invited Jesus to dine with him

_____ 5. one of the titles given to the Messiah

_____ 6. a city in Samaria where Jesus met the woman at the well

_____ 7. complained that her sister didn't help her prepare a meal for Jesus

_____ 8. was so short that he had to climb a tree to see Jesus through the crowd

_____ 9. a village not far from Jerusalem

_____ 10. the chief collector of taxes in Jericho

Multiple Choice

Directions: For each numbered item, circle the letter beside the choice (A, B, C, or D) that best answers the question or completes the statement. Circle only one choice per item. Each correct answer is worth 6 points. 60 possible points.

1. Which of the following events in the Old Testament was a foreshadowing of Christ's sacrifice on the Cross?

A. the flood in the days of Noah
B. Jacob's wrestling with the angel
C. the sacrifice of the Passover lamb
D. the appearance of the manna in the wilderness

2. What was the lesson of Jesus' story about the woman searching for the lost coin?

A. God treasures the lost sinner and searches for him.
B. God wants us to keep up with our money.
C. Every little bit helps.
D. Cleanliness is next to godliness.

3. In Jesus' story about the wayward son, how did the father treat the son who had sinned so terribly but at last repented?

A. He told him to go away, because he was no longer welcome at home.
B. He welcomed him home with new clothes and a celebration.
C. He refused to speak to him.
D. He allowed him to come back, but only as a servant, not as a son.

4. Why did the scribes and Pharisees bring to Jesus the woman caught in adultery?

A. They thought they could trick him into saying the wrong thing.
B. The woman was widely known as a sinner, and they wanted her to be punished.
C. They were hoping Jesus would teach her about forgiveness.
D. They wanted the people to see the wisdom of Jesus.

5. When Jesus said, "Unless a man is born again of water and the Holy Spirit, he cannot enter the kingdom of heaven," He was talking about:

A. making a profession of faith in God.
B. getting saved.
C. the Sacrament of Baptism.
D. the Sacrament of Confirmation.

6. Which woman named Mary appears frequently in the Gospel accounts, since she traveled with Jesus and served Him as a member of His band of disciples?

A. Mary the mother of Jesus
B. Mary of Bethany
C. Mary Magdalene
D. Mary of Jerusalem

7. How did Jesus respond to Martha's complaint about Mary?

A. He rebuked Mary for not helping Martha.
B. He rebuked Martha because she was always complaining.
C. He brought Martha and Mary together and told them to work it out with each other.
D. He told Martha that she was anxious about many things, but only one thing was important.

8. What did Jesus say to the woman who came to Him as He was dining and washed His feet with her tears?

A. "Your sins are forgiven."
B. "You must not touch me."
C. "You will be punished for your sins."
D. "Why have you come to Me?"

9. Why did the crowd murmur against Jesus when He announced that He would dine with Zacchaeus?

A. They wanted Jesus to dine with them instead.
B. They thought Jesus shouldn't be the guest of a man they considered a sinner.
C. It was a Sabbath, and they thought that Jesus should be fasting.
D. All of the above.

10. What can we learn about sharing our faith from Jesus' example when He spoke to the woman at the well?

A. We should tell others that we all need Christ, the "living water" bringing us eternal life.
B. Like Jesus, we shouldn't be afraid to cross social and religious boundaries to talk about God.
C. Like Jesus, we shouldn't be afraid to challenge other people's thinking and their way of life.
D. All of the above.

CHAPTER 5
Christ, the Great Teacher

Textbook pages: 67–79
Perfect score: 100

Your Score: _____

Matching

Directions: In each blank beside a phrase, write the letter of the term that is described by that phrase. Each item is worth 5 points. 25 possible points.

A. Beatitudes
B. Abraham's bosom
C. parables
D. Lazarus
E. Good Samaritan

_____ 1. teachings that compare the things of God to things from everyday life

_____ 2. a poor but good man who died and received his reward from God

_____ 3. helped a stranger who had been robbed and beaten

_____ 4. the place of rest after death for those who are faithful

_____ 5. Jesus' teaching about the actions and attitudes that God blesses

Multiple Choice

Directions: For each numbered item, circle the letter beside the choice (A, B, C, or D) that best answers the question or completes the statement. Circle only one choice per item. Each correct answer is worth 5 points. 75 possible points.

1. If the Son of God became Man in order to suffer and die for us on the Cross, why did He spend three years of His public life preaching?

A. According to Roman law, He had to be a certain age before He could die on a cross.
B. If He didn't teach us how to live a holy life, through ignorance we would fall back into our sins.
C. If He had died on the Cross without preaching, the scribes and Pharisees would have rejected Him.
D. If He had spent twenty years preaching, people would have gotten tired of listening to Him.

2. The Beatitudes are part of a longer homily that Jesus preached called:

A. the parable of the Good Shepherd.
B. the Living Waters sermon.
C. the Homily by the Sea.
D. the Sermon on the Mount.

3. Which of the following is *not* one of the Beatitudes?

A. "Blessed are the pure in heart, for they will see God."
B. "Blessed are the peacemakers, for they will be called children of God."
C. "Blessed are the meek, for they will become courageous."
D. "Blessed are the merciful, for they will obtain mercy."

4. When the disciples asked Jesus to teach them how to pray, what prayer did He teach them?

A. one of the Psalms in the Bible
B. the "Glory Be"
C. the "Hail Mary"
D. the "Our Father"

5. When Jesus began preaching, "Repent, for the kingdom of heaven is at hand!" how did some people misunderstand Him?

A. They thought that He had the wrong timing for the kingdom to come.
B. They thought He meant that the Roman Empire was the kingdom of heaven.
C. They thought He intended to establish an earthly kingdom instead of a spiritual one.
D. All of the above.

6. What lesson did Jesus say we can learn from the birds and the flowers?

A. God will provide for us what we need, so we don't have to worry.
B. Nothing lasts forever.
C. Beauty is in the eye of the beholder.
D. Creativity is part of God's nature.

7. What was Jesus' answer when Peter asked Him, "How often must I forgive my brother who sins against me?"

A. three times
B. seven times
C. ten times
D. seventy times seven times

8. What is "the Golden Rule" that Jesus taught?

A. "Love the Lord your God with all your mind, heart, soul, and strength."
B. "Do not judge, so that you will not be judged."
C. "All that you want others to do to you, do also to them."
D. "It is more blessed to give than to receive."

9. When Jesus wanted to teach us who it is that we should consider our neighbor, He replied with a parable known as:

A. the parable of the good Samaritan.
B. the parable of the loaves and fishes.
C. the parable of the rich man and the poor man.
D. the parable of the mustard seed.

10. What was Jesus warning us about in the parable of Lazarus and the rich man?

A. Jesus was warning us against neglecting those who are in need.
B. Jesus was warning that some of those who heard His message would refuse to believe in Him.
C. Both A and B.
D. None of the above.

11. What did Jesus say we must do when we are persecuted for our faith in Him?

A. We should be glad and rejoice, for our reward is great in heaven.
B. We should fight against those who persecute us.
C. We should persecute them instead.
D. All of the above.

12. Why did Jesus sometimes spend the whole night alone in a deserted place?

A. Whenever He felt ill, He wanted to be alone.
B. He sometimes lost His way as He was traveling from town to town.
C. He was angry with His disciples and wanted to get away from them.
D. He wanted to pray in solitude.

13. In the parable about the servant whose debt was forgiven by the king, why did the king become furious with the servant?

A. The servant owed the king so much money that he would never be able to pay it back.
B. The servant demanded that the king forgive his debt.
C. Though the king had forgiven the servant's debt, the servant refused to forgive the much smaller debt of his fellow servant.
D. The servant insisted that it wasn't his fault that he was in debt to the king.

14. What did Jesus have to say to those who are afraid that if they give to others, they won't have enough for themselves?

A. "Give, and it will be given to you."
B. "Give only to those who can repay you one day."
C. "Give only what you have extra."
D. "Lend instead of giving, so you will get it back."

15. What did Jesus teach about marriage?

A. Husbands and wives should remain married as long as they feel love for each other.
B. What God has joined together, let no one tear apart.
C. Married life is always full of joy and peace.
D. The family that prays together, stays together.

CHAPTER 6
Christ Works Miracles

Textbook pages: 81–88
Perfect score: 100

Your Score: _____

Matching

Directions: In each blank beside a phrase, write the letter of the term that is described by that phrase. Each item is worth 4 points. 20 possible points.

A. Cana
B. Peter
C. the apostles
D. Andrew
E. Mary the mother of Jesus

_____ 1. asked Jesus to help the hosts at a wedding feast

_____ 2. brought to Jesus the loaves and fishes of a young boy

_____ 3. walked on water with Jesus

_____ 4. received the loaves and fishes from Jesus to give out to the multitude

_____ 5. a town in Galilee

Multiple Choice

Directions: For each numbered item, circle the letter beside the choice (A, B, C, or D) that best answers the question or completes the statement. Circle only one choice per item. Each correct answer is worth 8 points. 80 possible points.

1. How could the people know that Jesus was truly speaking for God?

A. They knew Jesus must be speaking for God because they were so pleased with what He said.
B. They had a warm feeling in their hearts whenever Jesus spoke, so they knew the Holy Spirit was confirming what Jesus said.
C. The scribes and the Pharisees told them that Jesus was in fact God's Son.
D. The miracles He performed were the evidence God provided to show that Jesus was His divine Son.

2. The first of the miracles that Jesus performed took place in:

A. Jerusalem.
B. Nazareth.
C. Bethany.
D. Cana.

3. What did Mary say about Jesus to the waiters at the wedding feast?

A. "Just watch my Son work a miracle."
B. "Do whatever He tells you."
C. "He is displeased that the wine is running out."
D. "He will buy some more wine so that you won't run out."

4. Why did Jesus curse the fig tree?

A. Jesus was impatient because He was hungry and wanted to eat right away.
B. The fig tree belonged to a Pharisee.
C. Jesus wanted the disciples to know that the same divine power that had miraculously withered the fig tree could also work on their behalf if they had faith.
D. Jesus thought figs were unhealthy to eat.

5. Why didn't Jesus send away the crowds who pressed Him with their demands, even though He was weary and grieving?

A. He knew they were like sheep without a shepherd, and they needed Him.
B. He knew His disciples could handle the situation for Him.
C. If He sent them away, they would complain about Him to the scribes and Pharisees.
D. He knew that even if He told them to go away, they wouldn't do it anyway.

6. How did Jesus feed a multitude of thousands with only five barley loaves and two fishes?

A. He sent the apostles into the nearby villages to buy additional food.
B. He used a supply of extra food that He and the apostles always carried with them as they travelled.
C. The people had brought food with them, so they ended up sharing what they brought with one another.
D. He worked a miracle by multiplying the food so that there was more than enough.

7. How did Jesus save the apostles from drowning in the Sea of Galilee when their boat was battered by a raging storm?

A. He showed them how to handle the boat so that it wouldn't sink.
B. He helped them row to shore quickly, before it could sink.
C. He rebuked the wind and the raging sea, and immediately the storm ended.
D. He prayed that the waves wouldn't be able to sink the boat.

8. How did Jesus get from the shore to the apostles when they were in a boat out on the Sea of Galilee?

A. He waved at them from the shore so that they would row over to take Him on board.
B. He prayed for a great wind to drive them to the shore where He was waiting.
C. He climbed into a small boat and rowed out to them on the sea.
D. He walked on the water out to the boat.

9. When the apostles in the boat first saw Jesus from a distance, how did they respond?

A. They were terrified because they thought He was a ghost.
B. They shut their eyes because they thought their eyes were playing tricks on them.
C. They pinched themselves because they thought they were dreaming.
D. They recognized Him, so they bowed down in the boat to worship Him.

10. Why did Peter begin sinking into the water?

A. Even though he was a fisherman, he had never learned how to swim.
B. When he looked at how strong the wind was, his faith gave way to doubt.
C. A large wave knocked him overboard.
D. He was a good swimmer, but the waves were so high that they overcame him.

CHAPTER 7
Christ, the Friend of the Sick

Textbook pages: 89–98
Perfect score: 100

Your Score: _____

Matching

Directions: In each blank beside a phrase, write the letter of the term that is described by that phrase. Each item is worth 5 points. 20 possible points.

A. Capernaum
B. centurion
C. Pool of Siloam
D. leprosy
E. Bartimaeus

_____ 1. a blind man waiting along the roadside who was healed by Jesus

_____ 2. a place in Jerusalem where Jesus sent a blind man to receive his sight

_____ 3. a town where the people brought to Jesus all who were ill or possessed by demons

_____ 4. an officer in command of Roman soldiers

_____ 5. now known as Hansen's disease

Multiple Choice

Directions: For each numbered item, circle the letter beside the choice (A, B, C, or D) that best answers the question or completes the statement. Circle only one choice per item. Each correct answer is worth 8 points. 80 possible points.

1. What did Our Lord's miracles of healing mean to the people?

A. They were evidence that Jesus was God's divine Son.
B. They were signs of Our Lord's compassion for those who were afflicted.
C. They gave great consolation to the people, showing them that God cared about them.
D. All of the above.

2. Why was Jesus amazed at the words of the Roman centurion?

A. He didn't expect a Roman to speak Aramaic.
B. He was surprised that a military officer would care so much about a lowly servant boy.
C. Even though the centurion was a pagan, he understood well the power and authority of the Savior.
D. Most Roman officers would have ordered Jesus to help them instead of requesting His help.

3. How did the paralyzed man get to Jesus through a crowded house so that he could be healed?

A. His friends lifted him onto the roof, opened a hole in it, and lowered him down to Jesus.
B. He cried out so loudly that Jesus heard him above the crowd and told them to bring the man to Him.
C. Jesus had heard about the paralyzed man, so He left the house to search for him.
D. Jesus healed the man from a distance so that he could walk through the crowd to come to Him.

4. Why were the Pharisees angry that Jesus told the paralyzed man his sins were forgiven?

A. They insisted that only God can forgive sins, and they didn't believe that Jesus was God.
B. They knew the man's sins were many, and they wanted the man to pay for his sins.
C. They thought that they themselves should be the ones to tell the man that his sins were forgiven.
D. They didn't believe in forgiveness of sins.

5. How did the woman who had suffered from a flow of blood for twelve years come to be healed?

A. She prayed, and God healed her as she slept one night.
B. She came to Jesus by night, when the crowd was gone, and asked Him to heal her.
C. She worked her way through the crowd, touched the hem of Jesus' clothes, and was cured.
D. The doctors finally figured out how to cure her.

6. What did Bartimaeus do when people told him to stop calling out for Jesus to help him?

A. He called out all the more loudly until Jesus heard him and invited him to come forward.
B. He stopped calling Jesus and went home in disappointment.
C. He struck the people with his staff and told them to mind their own business.
D. He became silent and sat by the road, weeping.

7. How did Jesus reply when the apostles asked about a blind man, "Who has sinned, this man or his parents, that he would be born blind?"

A. Jesus said that the man was being punished for his own sins.
B. Jesus said that the man was being punished for the sins of his parents.
C. Jesus said that the man was being punished both for his own sins and for the sins of his parents.
D. Jesus said that neither the man nor his parents had sinned; he was born blind so that the power of God could be demonstrated in him.

8. Why did the Pharisees object to Jesus' healing of the blind man?

A. He did it on a Sabbath, and they insisted that making mud and healing someone were forms of work forbidden on the Sabbath.
B. They wanted both the man and his parents to be punished for their sins.
C. They thought it was undignified for Jesus to use mud made from dirt and spittle to heal the man.
D. They wanted the people to think that they were the only ones who had the power to heal the sick.

9. How did Jesus heal the man who couldn't hear or speak?

A. Jesus said simply, "Be healed," and the man was healed.
B. Jesus told the man to go show himself to the priest, and when the man did, he was healed.
C. Jesus put His fingers into the man's ears, then spit, touched the man's tongue, and said, "Be opened!"
D. Jesus gave the man a powerful medicine that opened his ears and loosed his tongue.

10. Of the ten lepers who were healed by Jesus, how many took the time to thank Him?

A. All of them took the time to thank Jesus for working such a great miracle.
B. Five of them were children, and they were the only ones who thanked Jesus.
C. They were all so excited that none of them took the time to thank Jesus.
D. Only one of them thanked Jesus, and he was a Samaritan.

Chapter 8
Christ Casts Out Demons and Raises the Dead

Textbook pages: 99–110
Perfect score: 100

Your Score: _____

Matching

Directions: In each blank beside a phrase, write the letter of the term that is described by that phrase. Each item is worth 4 points. 40 possible points.

A. legion
B. Nain
C. Lazarus
D. Tyre
E. Caiaphas
F. Martha
G. Jairus
H. Gerasenes
I. Decapolis
J. son of David

_____ 1. a Canaanite city in the time of Jesus

_____ 2. the region of ten cities where the man freed from a demon told what Jesus had done for him

_____ 3. the ruler of the synagogue at Capernaum

_____ 4. a high priest who opposed Jesus

_____ 5. a sister of Lazarus

_____ 6. a Gentile people who lived across the sea from Capernaum

_____ 7. a Roman military term for a company of thousands of soldiers

_____ 8. Jesus' friend, whom He raised from the dead

_____ 9. one of the titles of Christ

_____ 10. a little town in Galilee

Multiple Choice

Directions: For each numbered item, circle the letter beside the choice (A, B, C, or D) that best answers the question or completes the statement. Circle only one choice per item. Each correct answer is worth 6 points. 60 possible points.

1. What were the symptoms of those persons whom Jesus delivered from demon possession?

A. The person had times when he wasn't in control of himself, and the demon took over his speech and his body movements.
B. The demon might torment his victim, inflicting pain, throwing him around, or causing him to suffer some terrible illness.
C. Both A and B above.
D. None of the above.

2. What evidence do we have in the Gospels that the demons Jesus encountered in His ministry recognized Him as the holy Son of God?

A. When the demons spoke to Jesus, they themselves admitted that they knew who He was.
B. When Jesus commanded them, the demons obeyed.
C. The demons were afraid of Jesus.
D. All of the above.

3. How do we know that the Gerasene man was truly possessed by a demon and not simply mentally ill?

A. As the Son of God, Jesus would not have mistaken a mental illness for demonic possession.
B. A mental illness cannot be cast out of a man into a herd of pigs.
C. Both A and B above.
D. None of the above.

4. Which of the following is *not* a reason why the Gerasenes wanted Jesus to leave after He cast the demons out of the man who had been possessed?

A. The Gerasenes were afraid of Jesus' power.
B. The Gerasenes wanted Jesus to help demon-possessed people in other cities as well.
C. The Gerasenes who owned the swine resented having lost them.
D. The Gerasenes who were tending the swine herd were terrified and stirred up the others against Him.

5. How did the father of the demon-possessed boy respond when Jesus said to him, "All things are possible to the one who believes"?

A. He said to Jesus, "Are you certain of that?"
B. He said to Jesus, "Show me Your power so that I can believe in You."
C. He said to Jesus, "I'm sorry, but I simply can't believe."
D. He said to Jesus, "I do believe; help my unbelief!"

6. Why couldn't the disciples cast the demon out of the boy?

A. They couldn't do it because of their lack of faith.
B. They couldn't do it because only Jesus could cast out demons.
C. They couldn't do it because they didn't know what to say to the demons.
D. They couldn't do it because the boy's father wouldn't let them.

7. Why didn't Jesus respond right away to the woman who begged him to deliver her daughter from demon possession?

A. Jesus wanted to test her faith and her persistence.
B. It was an inconvenient time for Jesus to respond.
C. The woman wasn't Jewish, so Jesus didn't want to help her.
D. Jesus didn't hear her request because He was busy teaching the disciples.

8. What did Jesus mean when He told the mourners surrounding Jairus' daughter, "Don't weep. The girl isn't dead, but only sleeping"?

A. Jesus meant that the doctors had been mistaken, and the girl was actually in a coma.
B. Jesus meant that the girl was only pretending to be dead.
C. Jesus was just trying to make the mourners feel better.
D. Because Jesus knew He would raise the girl from the dead, her condition was like a sleep from which she would be awakened.

9. Why were Mary and Martha disappointed in Jesus?

A. The sisters thought that Jesus could have healed Lazarus without even traveling to Bethany.
B. The sisters thought that Jesus didn't really love Lazarus after all.
C. Jesus had waited several days to come to Lazarus after hearing that he was sick, and the sisters were certain that if Jesus had come sooner to heal him, Lazarus wouldn't have died.
D. The sisters thought that Jesus shouldn't have let Lazarus get sick in the first place.

10. How could Jesus' enemy Caiaphas prophesy, without realizing it, that Jesus was the Savior?

A. The Holy Spirit had Caiaphas utter the prophecy while he was sleeping.
B. The Holy Spirit placed Caiaphas into a trance while he was prophesying.
C. Caiaphas wasn't actually speaking for himself, but rather the Holy Spirit was speaking through him because he was the high priest.
D. The Holy Spirit made Caiaphas prophesy in a foreign language that he couldn't understand.

CHAPTER 9
Christ, the Friend of the Poor

Textbook pages: 111–119
Perfect score: 100

Your Score: _____

Multiple Choice

Directions: For each numbered item, circle the letter beside the choice (A, B, C, or D) that best answers the question or completes the statement. Circle only one choice per item. Each correct answer is worth 10 points. 100 possible points.

1. How did Jesus experience poverty?

A. Jesus was born into a poor family.
B. Jesus and His apostles depended on the charity of the people for their bodily needs.
C. Jesus would send His disciples into a field to gather the wheat that the owners had left behind for the poor.
D. All of the above.

2. Who are the poor in spirit that Jesus talked about in the Sermon on the Mount?

A. The poor in spirit are those who don't have much interest in spiritual matters.
B. The poor in spirit are those who are wealthy but think they need more wealth.
C. The poor in spirit are those whose hearts are not set on the things of this world.
D. The poor in spirit are those who are downcast.

3. Why did the rich young man who came to Jesus seeking advice turn away in sorrow after Jesus told him what to do?

A. Jesus told the young man to give away his possessions and become a disciple, but the young man didn't have the courage to give them up.
B. Jesus told the young man that he could never be a disciple because he didn't have enough faith.
C. Jesus told the young man that he would have to spend all his money in supporting the disciples.
D. Jesus told him to go away because He didn't like rich people.

4. What did Jesus mean when He said, "It's easier for a camel to squeeze through the eye of a needle, than for a rich man to enter the kingdom of heaven"?

A. Jesus was making a little joke so that His listeners would not be so serious about spiritual matters.
B. Since a camel can't really squeeze through the eye of a needle, Jesus meant that rich people cannot be saved.

question continued on next page ➡

C. Jesus was trying to make poor people feel better about their condition.

D. Jesus meant that as long as a rich man puts his faith in what he possesses, he won't be able to gain the happiness of heaven.

5. Why did Jesus say that the widow who gave to God only two little copper coins had given more than everyone else?

A. Jesus knew that the widow had come to the Temple earlier that day to give some silver that her husband had left behind.

B. The coins were actually rare antique coins that were worth more than gold.

C. The others had so much money that they could give to God some of what they had to spare, but she was poor and had given everything she had.

D. The coins were copper on the outside, but they were gold on the inside.

6. What was "the Price of the Soul"?

A. It was the ransom paid to free someone who had been kidnapped.

B. It was a half-shekel Temple tax required by the Law of Moses.

C. It was the typical purchase price of a slave.

D. It was the dowry money paid to a bridegroom by the family of his bride.

7. How did Jesus instruct Peter to get the money needed for their taxes?

A. Jesus told Peter to borrow the money from one of their wealthy disciples.

B. Jesus told Peter that as he went to pay their taxes, he would find a coin lying somewhere along the road that he could use for that purpose.

C. Jesus told Peter that if he would go fishing and look in the mouth of the first fish he caught, he would find a coin he could use to pay their taxes.

D. Jesus told Peter to catch some fish and then sell them to get the money to pay their taxes.

8. Why did Jesus tell the parable of the rich man who decided to build larger barns to store up all his goods, but died before he could carry out his plan?

A. Jesus wanted to emphasize how quickly life passes away, with the loss of all our possessions.

B. Jesus wanted to warn rich people that they could not enter the kingdom of heaven.

C. Jesus thought that it was foolish to build barns.

D. All of the above.

9. Which of the following did Jesus *not* say will take place in the Great Judgment at the end of the world?

A. He will sit on His throne of glory, and all the nations will be gathered together before Him.

B. All people will be welcomed into heaven, no matter how they lived their lives on earth.

C. The sun and the moon will be darkened, and the stars will fall from heaven.

D. All people will see Him coming in the clouds of heaven with great power and majesty.

10. When Jesus talked about Judgment Day, who were those He called "blessed of My Father" who would be rewarded in heaven?

A. The ones who had called Jesus their Lord.
B. The ones who had never sinned.
C. The ones who had become priests and deacons.
D. The ones who had cared for those in need.

CHAPTER 10
Christ Founds His Church

Textbook pages: 121–137
Perfect score: 100 Your Score: _____

Multiple Choice

Directions: For each numbered item, circle the letter beside the choice (A, B, C, or D) that best answers the question or completes the statement. Circle only one choice per item. Each correct answer is worth 5 points. 100 possible points.

1. Why did Jesus establish the Church?

A. Through the Church, the kingdom of God that Jesus founded would extend throughout the earth.
B. Through the Church, after His ascension into heaven Jesus could remain on earth in a new way and continue the work He had begun.
C. Both A and B above.
D. None of the above.

2. Why did Jesus appoint the apostles?

A. The apostles were part of the foundation of the Church that Jesus intended to establish.
B. Jesus needed twelve men to help him manage the money and properties that people gave Him.
C. The apostles were useful for managing the crowds and turning away the people who didn't really need to see Jesus.
D. Jesus appointed twelve of His male relatives as apostles to give them a special status among His disciples.

3. Which of the apostles was the "rock" on which Jesus built His Church, who received from Him the keys to the kingdom of heaven?

A. John
B. Peter
C. James
D. Matthew

4. What did Jesus mean when He said to Peter, "Whatever you will bind on earth will be bound also in heaven; and whatever you will loose on earth will be loosed also in heaven"?

A. Jesus was saying that after His ascension into heaven, Peter would become the new Messiah.
B. Together with the rest of the apostles, Peter would have the authority from Christ to

question continued on next page →

say what was right and what was wrong, what was true and what was false.

C. Both A and B above.

D. None of the above.

5. What was the main lesson of Jesus' parable of the vineyard?

A. Just as a vineyard gives us grapes for wine, Jesus gives us His Blood in the Eucharist.

B. The Church needs the Word of God just as a vineyard needs sunshine.

C. Just as grapes are pressed to make wine, the Church will be pressed by adversity.

D. We must remain deeply connected to Christ if we are to be spiritually fruitful.

6. Why did Jesus compare Himself to a shepherd, and His followers to sheep?

A. A shepherd leads His sheep to water and pasture.

B. A shepherd protects His sheep from predators.

C. A shepherd knows His sheep well, and they know His voice.

D. All of the above.

7. What did Jesus mean when He said, "I have other sheep as well that are not of this sheepfold"?

A. His flock of sheep included people who weren't following Him at the time.

B. His flock of sheep would include not only the Jewish people, but the Gentiles as well.

C. His flock of sheep included the living as well as the dead.

D. All of the above.

8. Who are the "weeds" in Jesus' parable of the weeds in the field?

A. the members of His Church who fail to be true to His teaching and who lead sinful lives

B. the Gentiles who settled among the Jews in ancient Palestine

C. the scribes and the Pharisees

D. the people who refuse to become Christians and enter the Church

9. According to the parable of the weeds in the field, when does God separate the "wheat" from the "weeds"?

A. God will separate them at the end of the world.

B. God separates them each day, as He makes it clear to all which people are "wheat" and which are "weeds."

C. God separated them when Jesus rose from the dead.

D. God separated them on the day of Pentecost.

10. Which other parable that Jesus told teaches the same lesson as the parable of the weeds in the field?

A. the parable of the mustard seed

B. the parable of the fishing net

question continued on next page ➝

C. the parable of the lost coin

D. the parable of the pearl of great price

11. Why did Jesus compare the Church to a mustard seed?

A. Like a mustard seed, the Church produces much sweet fruit.

B. Like a mustard seed, the Church must remain underground.

C. Like a mustard seed, the Church thrives only in rocky soil.

D. Like a mustard seed, the Church starts out small, but over time puts out its branches, grows large, and provides a home for many.

12. What is the main lesson of Jesus' parable of the treasure hidden in a field?

A. We cannot always find our way to God, because He is hidden.

B. We must be ready to make every sacrifice to possess the kingdom of heaven.

C. The value of a treasure is in the eyes of the beholder.

D. We must cultivate the field of life to discover its treasure.

13. Which other parable that Jesus told teaches the same lesson as the parable of the treasure hidden in a field?

A. the parable of the mustard seed

B. the parable of the fishing net

C. the parable of the lost coin

D. the parable of the pearl of great price

14. What is the lesson of Jesus' parable about the barren fig tree?

A. Those who haven't produced spiritual fruit just need more time.

B. Some people aren't made to produce spiritual fruit.

C. If we continue to reject God's grace, eventually we'll face His judgment.

D. Spiritual fruit can sometimes be poisoned.

15. What point was Jesus making when He said, "Whoever does the will of My Father in heaven is My brother and sister and mother"?

A. Jesus was saying that those who do God's will are members of His family, the Church.

B. Jesus was saying that His mother is just like everyone else and has no special privileges.

C. Jesus was saying that the people who came to Him in need were more important than His mother.

D. All of the above.

16. What was the lesson of Jesus' parable of the talents?

A. We must cultivate our particular talents so that our contribution to God's kingdom will be multiplied.

B. Not everyone called to be members of Christ's Church will receive the same graces.

C. If we fail to develop a talent, we could eventually lose it.

D. All of the above.

17. Why did Jesus tell the parable of the good and bad soils?

A. He wanted to warn the people against the scribes and Pharisees.
B. He wanted the apostles to stop wasting their time preaching to the crowds.
C. He wanted to see which of the people had "good soil," and which had "bad soil."
D. He was explaining why some people heard His message and changed their lives, while others didn't.

18. What was the main lesson of Jesus' parable about the wise and foolish maidens?

A. Some people will always be irresponsible, even in the Church.
B. We must always share what we have with others.
C. We must be ready at all times to give an account of ourselves to Christ, our Judge.
D. Our life in Christ will be full of surprises, but we shouldn't be concerned about that.

19. When Jesus taught about the Bread of Life, what was He talking about?

A. the manna God sent the Israelites in the wilderness
B. Himself
C. the people of God
D. the Scripture

20. When Jesus said that His disciples would have to eat His flesh and drink His blood, what did He mean?

A. We must receive the Eucharist, but it is only a symbol of His Body and Blood.
B. To eat His flesh and drink His blood, we need only remember His death on the Cross.
C. To eat His flesh and drink His blood, we need only pray to Him.
D. We must receive the Eucharist, which is truly His Body and Blood.

CHAPTER 11
The Disciples Struggle to Understand

Textbook pages: 139–146
Perfect score: 100

Your Score: _____

Matching

Directions: In each blank beside a phrase, write the letter of the term that is described by that phrase. You may match more than one description to a single term. Each item is worth 2 points. 20 possible points.

A. Moses and Elijah
B. Peter, James, and John
C. Tabor
D. Peter
E. James and John

_____ 1. their mother wanted them to have a high place in Jesus' kingdom

_____ 2. wanted to bring down divine judgment on those who mistreated them

_____ 3. nicknamed by Jesus the "Sons of Thunder"

_____ 4. watched as Jesus was transfigured in glory

_____ 5. the place where Jesus was transfigured in glory

_____ 6. wanted to set up three tents on the mountaintop

_____ 7. appeared alongside Jesus at His transfiguration

_____ 8. one of the highest mountains in Palestine

_____ 9. Jesus once said to him, "Get behind Me, Satan!"

_____ 10. the apostle who usually spoke for all the rest

Multiple Choice

Directions: For each numbered item, circle the letter beside the choice (A, B, C, or D) that best answers the question or completes the statement. Circle only one choice per item. Each correct answer is worth 10 points. 80 possible points.

1. Why did the apostles misunderstand Jesus' teaching about the kingdom of heaven?

A. Jesus had never really explained to them what He was talking about.
B. Jesus wanted to keep His message a mystery until after His resurrection.
C. When Jesus spoke of the kingdom of heaven, they thought of an earthly kingdom.
D. They thought that the kingdom had been established long before their time.

2. What did Jesus mean when He said, "If anyone wants to come after Me, let him deny himself, and take up his cross, and follow Me"?

A. Jesus knew His disciples would have to make their own crosses to imitate what He would do for them.
B. Jesus was asking His disciples to surrender to the Roman authorities when He was arrested, so they could die alongside Him.
C. Jesus was making it clear that being His disciple is not always easy.
D. All of the above.

3. How did Jesus respond when the mother of some of the apostles wanted her sons to have a high position in His kingdom?

A. Jesus granted her request.
B. Jesus said they were not worthy of such an honor.
C. Jesus said they would first have to be tested to see whether they were worthy of such an honor.
D. Jesus said that it was not in His power to answer her request.

4. Why did the Samaritans refuse to provide hospitality to Jesus and the apostles?

A. Most Samaritans wanted nothing to do with the Jews, and the Jews felt the same way about the Samaritans.
B. None of the Samaritan inns were large enough to hold such a large group.
C. It was a Samaritan holiday, so all their inns were full.
D. Jesus and the apostles couldn't pay the high price that the Samaritans demanded.

5. How did the "Sons of Thunder" respond to the Samaritans' refusal to provide hospitality?

A. They asked Jesus to forgive the Samaritans.
B. They wanted to call down fire from heaven to destroy the Samaritans.
C. They said they would travel through the night so they wouldn't need lodging.
D. They wanted Jesus Himself to go demand hospitality from the Samaritans, threatening God's punishment if they said no.

6. What was Jesus' attitude toward children?

A. He said that His disciples had to receive the kingdom of God like a child.
B. He invited children to come to Him for His blessing.
C. He warned of a terrible judgment for those who lead children into sin.
D. All of the above.

7. Why were some of Jesus' followers upset by His claim to be the Bread of Life from heaven?

A. They knew Mary and Joseph, so they insisted that Jesus had come into the world as any other child comes, rather than descending from heaven.
B. They insisted that the true Bread of Life was the Scripture.
C. They believed that they themselves were the true Bread of Life.
D. They thought that the true Bread of Life was the manna God had sent to their ancestors in the wilderness.

8. What happened when Jesus was transfigured?

A. His appearance was transformed, so that His face shone like the sun, and His clothing became as bright as lightning.
B. Two saints from the Old Testament appeared and began to talk with Jesus about His death that would soon take place in Jerusalem.
C. A bright cloud overshadowed them and a voice spoke from heaven.
D. All of the above.

PART THREE

CHAPTER 12
The Enemies of Christ

Textbook pages: 147–161
Perfect score: 100

Your Score: _____

Matching

Directions: In each blank beside a phrase, write the letter of the term that is described by that phrase. Each item is worth 4 points. 20 possible points.

A. Bethsaida
B. parchment
C. I AM
D. Ephraim
E. Herod

_____ 1. a little town about sixteen miles northeast of Jerusalem

_____ 2. a name of God

_____ 3. a pool in Jerusalem where people were sometimes healed of their illnesses

_____ 4. thought that Jesus might be John the Baptist returned from the dead

_____ 5. a long scroll of animal skin specially prepared as a surface to write on

Multiple Choice

Directions: For each numbered item, circle the letter beside the choice (A, B, C, or D) that best answers the question or completes the statement. Circle only one choice per item. Each correct answer is worth 4 points. 80 possible points.

1. Why did the Pharisees so often earn Jesus' rebuke?

A. Many of the Pharisees were guilty of hypocrisy, which showed itself in various ways.

B. The Pharisees were careless about performing all the outward actions that the Law of Moses commanded.
C. The Pharisees denied several important truths of doctrine, such as the resurrection of the dead and the existence of angels.
D. The Pharisees refused to attend the Temple or the synagogues.

2. What did Jesus mean when He said, "When you give alms, don't let your left hand know what your right hand is doing"?

A. We should give only a limited amount of alms—one handful instead of two.
B. We shouldn't be trying to tell everyone about how generous we are.
C. Both A and B.
D. None of the above.

3. In Jesus' story of the Pharisee and the tax collector praying in the Temple, why did the tax collector go home justified by God, but the Pharisee did not?

A. The tax collector had become a disciple of Jesus, but the Pharisee had not.
B. The tax collector had fasted and given alms, but the Pharisee had not.
C. The tax collector recognized and confessed his own sinfulness, but the Pharisee did not.
D. The tax collector had given all his money to the poor, but the Pharisee had not.

4. Why were the Pharisees wrong in their attitude toward the Sabbath?

A. They were lax in observing the Sabbath, breaking the Law of Moses.
B. They were so strict about enforcing the Sabbath law that they considered anything done on the Sabbath other than worship or rest to be sinful.
C. They engaged in so many forms of recreation on the Sabbath that they forgot it should be a day of rest.
D. They tried to make Gentiles observe the Sabbath as well as Jews.

5. How were people sometimes healed in the pool in Jerusalem?

A. An angel sometimes came down into the pool to stir the water, and the first person who went into the pool after the stirring of the water was cured.
B. When those who were sick entered the pool, the high priest stood over them and prayed for them.
C. The waters were mixed with herbs that healed many ailments.
D. When the sick were baptized in the pool, they were often cured of their illness.

6. Why did some people become angry at Jesus after He healed the lame man?

A. He did it on a Sabbath day, and they considered healing ministry to be forbidden work on the Sabbath.
B. He did it on a Sabbath day, and Jesus had told the healed man to take up his bed and walk, which they considered to be forbidden work on the Sabbath.
C. They considered it blasphemous for Him to say that God was His Father, showing Himself equal to God.
D. All of the above.

7. What did Jesus say to the Pharisees who didn't want Him to heal a man with a withered hand on the Sabbath?

A. "Is it lawful on the Sabbath to do good or to do evil, to save life or to destroy it?"
B. "I will wait till another day to heal him so that you will not bother him."
C. "Which one among you is able to heal him as I can?"
D. "Leave us now, for of such as these is the kingdom of heaven."

8. What was the main lesson of the parable that Jesus told about the great banquet?

A. He wanted to show that feasting has God's blessing.
B. He wanted to show that only a few people have been invited to enter the kingdom of heaven.
C. He wanted the Pharisees to understand that no one has a right to the kingdom of heaven simply because he belongs to a certain nation or people.
D. All of the above.

9. In the parable of the great banquet, why did the servants go out to the highways searching for guests?

A. All the guests had lost their way and couldn't find the banquet hall.
B. The guests who were originally invited had failed to come, making excuses for their absence.
C. The guests had drunk too much wine and were wandering around outside on the highways.
D. The master of the feast had forgotten to send out invitations to the guests.

10. What did Jesus mean when He said that some religious leaders "strain out the gnat from their drink, but swallow the camel"?

A. They didn't follow the dietary restrictions on beverages commanded in the Law of Moses.
B. They spent too much time feasting and not enough time fasting.
C. Though they could be very exact in observing small details of the Law of Moses, they allowed many grave abuses in religious life.
D. They didn't offer generous hospitality to strangers.

11. Why did Jesus drive the moneychangers out of the Temple?

A. They had turned the House of God into a market place, and greed drove them to demand too much money for their services.
B. They kept all the money they made for themselves instead of giving some to the Temple treasury.
C. The people really didn't need the moneychangers' services, because they could pay for their Temple offerings with Roman coins if they wanted to do so.
D. The moneychangers were driving all the people away from the Temple.

12. What did Jesus mean when He said, "Destroy this Temple, and in three days I will raise it up"?

A. If the Romans destroyed the Temple, He had the power to rebuild it miraculously.
B. After He was put to death, the Temple of His body would be raised up on the third day.
C. If an earthquake destroyed the Temple, in three days He could rebuild it with the help of all the people.
D. All of the above.

13. Why was there no altar in the synagogue at Nazareth when Jesus visited?

A. Altars were expensive to purchase, and the people there were too poor to afford one.
B. The synagogue at Nazareth was still under construction at the time Jesus visited.
C. The altar had been removed for repairs at the time Jesus visited.
D. An altar is a place for offering sacrifices, and sacrifices were never offered in synagogues.

14. Why was the main body of the synagogue divided into two parts?

A. One part was reserved for the children, and the other for the adults.
B. One part was reserved for the Jews, and the other for the Gentiles.
C. One part was reserved for the men, and the other for the women.
D. One part was reserved for the Pharisees, and the other for everyone else.

15. In the synagogue, what was kept in a wooden chest covered with a veil?

A. a golden seven-branched candlestick
B. the rabbi's silver cup
C. the sacred books of Scripture
D. the high priest's vestments

16. What took place in a synagogue service?

A. the singing of Psalms
B. prayers
C. the reading of Scripture with instruction about its meaning
D. All of the above.

17. Why were the people in the synagogue of Jesus' hometown, Nazareth, angry with Him?

A. They were offended by His teaching.
B. He had told the Gentiles attending the service that they could sit alongside the Jews.
C. They were upset that He had left His mother alone while He traveled.
D. They thought only a rabbi should be allowed to read the Scripture and teach in the synagogue.

18. In addition to blasphemy, what charge did Jesus' opponents make against Him?

A. They said He was a fraud because the people He claimed to heal weren't really healed.
B. They said He lived an immoral life that led the people astray.
C. They said He was a Samaritan with a demon.
D. They said He was actually an Egyptian magician in disguise.

19. Which member of the Sanhedrin spoke up for Jesus when the council was plotting against Him?

A. Nicodemus
B. Joseph of Arimathea
C. Caiaphas
D. Ananaias

20. Why were the Pharisees afraid to have Jesus arrested and brought before the high priest on a charge of blasphemy?

A. They knew the high priest would dismiss the case.
B. They worried that the Romans would punish them for arresting Jesus.
C. He had never said anything that would allow them to charge Him with blasphemy.
D. Those who remained faithful followers of Jesus might riot if the religious leaders moved against Him.

CHAPTER 13
The Last Days of Christ's Ministry

Textbook pages: 163–172
Perfect score: 100

Your Score: _____

Matching

Directions: In each blank beside a phrase, write the letter of the term that is described by that phrase. You may match more than one description to a single term. Each item is worth 4 points. 40 possible points.

A. Hosanna
B. Bethphage
C. Mary of Bethany
D. Son of David
E. Philip and Andrew
F. Caiaphas
G. Judas Iscariot
H. Caesar
I. the Devil

_____ 1. a little town near the Mount of Olives

_____ 2. was in charge of the offerings that people gave the apostles

_____ 3. the Roman emperor

_____ 4. betrayed Jesus for thirty pieces of silver

_____ 5. means "Save us!"

_____ 6. the high priest who plotted Jesus' arrest and death

_____ 7. anointed Jesus' head and feet with an alabaster jar of ointment

_____ 8. the prince of this world

_____ 9. brought Gentiles to see Jesus

_____ 10. a name for the Messiah

Multiple Choice

Directions: For each numbered item, circle the letter beside the choice (A, B, C, or D) that best answers the question or completes the statement. Circle only one choice per item. Each correct answer is worth 6 points. 60 possible points.

1. Why was Judas indignant when Jesus' head and feet were anointed with an expensive alabaster jar of ointment?

A. He wanted to sell it and give the money to the poor instead.
B. He wanted to sell it and keep the money with the offerings, so he could steal it.
C. He thought that the woman was bothering Jesus, so he wanted her to go away.
D. He knew that not everyone liked the fragrance of the ointment, and it was filling the house.

2. When Jesus entered Jerusalem, why did the people crowd around Him with palm branches in their hands, crying out, "Hosanna"?

A. The people mistook Jesus for a visiting king from another country.
B. The scribes and Pharisees had instructed the people to receive Jesus this way so they could accuse Him of causing an uprising.
C. The Roman soldiers had instructed the people to receive Jesus this way so they could keep an eye on Him.
D. The people were welcoming Jesus as the Messiah, the royal descendant of King David.

3. Why did Jesus weep over Jerusalem?

A. The city was so beautiful, gleaming white in the brilliant sunlight, that it moved Him to tears.
B. He knew that the city would one day be destroyed by enemy forces as a divine judgment.
C. He wept tears of joy at the sight of His Father's house, the Temple.
D. All of the above.

4. Why were there a number of Gentiles in Jerusalem at the Passover feast?

A. They may have been converts to the Jewish faith who had come to worship.
B. There was a great deal of money to be made off the worshippers at the feast.
C. Jerusalem had a large native population of Gentiles.
D. The Gentiles enjoyed big celebrations as much as the Jews did.

5. What did Jesus mean when He said, "Unless a grain of wheat falls into the earth and dies, it remains alone; but if it dies, it bears much fruit"?

A. Jesus was reminding the farmers that they must remain diligent in their work.
B. Jesus was comparing His death and resurrection to the planting of wheat.
C. Both A and B above.
D. None of the above.

6. What effect did the Father's words from heaven have on the people who heard His voice?

A. The words strengthened the faith of Jesus' disciples and prepared them for what was coming.
B. Some among the crowds heard the sound, but said it was just thunder.
C. Some among the crowds thought an angel had spoken to Jesus.
D. All of the above.

7. Why did the religious leaders refuse to answer Jesus' question about whether the baptism of John was from heaven or merely from men?

A. They hadn't followed John, so they couldn't admit that God had sent him; but if they said that John wasn't sent by God, the people might stone them.
B. They refused to answer Jesus' question until He first answered their questions.
C. They were so busy arguing among themselves that they didn't even hear Jesus ask the question.
D. Jesus was from Nazareth, and they were too proud to debate with someone who came from Galilee instead of Judea.

8. Why did the Pharisees ask Jesus, "Is it lawful to give tribute to Caesar, or not?"

A. The Pharisees were worried because they didn't know whether it was sinful to pay tribute to the Roman emperor.
B. The Pharisees wanted to trick Jesus into angering either the Jews, who hated paying the tribute, or the Romans, who demanded that they pay it.
C. The Pharisees were poor, so they didn't want to pay the tribute unless it was truly necessary.
D. The Pharisees felt sorry for the poor, so they didn't want them to have to pay the tribute.

9. Why did the chief priest initially insist that Jesus shouldn't be arrested during the Passover festival?

A. The Passover was a sacred feast, and they would dishonor it by making an arrest.
B. There were so many people attending the Passover feast that it would be impossible to find Jesus in the great crowds.
C. Many people in the crowds attending the Passover feast might rise up and defend Jesus if anyone laid hands on Him.
D. The Law of Moses commanded that no one could be arrested during the Passover feast.

10. What price was Judas paid by the chief priests for betraying Jesus?

A. enough money to live on for a lifetime
B. enough money to make him the wealthiest man in Jerusalem
C. a hundred talents of gold
D. thirty pieces of silver

CHAPTER 14
Christ at the Last Supper and in the Garden

Textbook pages: 173–184
Perfect score: 100

Your Score: _____

Matching

Directions: In each blank beside a phrase, write the letter of the term that is described by that phrase. You may match more than one description to a single term. Each item is worth 4 points. 40 possible points.

A. Peter
B. Kidron
C. Malachi
D. Malchus
E. Mount of Olives
F. Judas
G. Gethsemane
H. Peter, James, and John

_____ 1. prophesied that the Sacrifice of the Mass would be offered throughout the world

_____ 2. Jesus said it would be better for him if he had never been born

_____ 3. means "olive press"

_____ 4. objected to Jesus' washing his feet

_____ 5. a brook beside the Mount of Olives

_____ 6. where the Garden of Gethsemane was located

_____ 7. the servant of the high priest who lost his right ear

_____ 8. used a sword in an attempt to protect Jesus from arrest

_____ 9. went to sleep while Jesus was praying in the garden

_____ 10. said he would die for Jesus

Multiple Choice

Directions: For each numbered item, circle the letter beside the choice (A, B, C, or D) that best answers the question or completes the statement. Circle only one choice per item. Each correct answer is worth 6 points. 60 possible points.

1. Which Jewish feast were Jesus and the apostles celebrating at the Last Supper?

A. the Feast of Pentecost
B. the Feast of Tabernacles
C. the Feast of Passover
D. the Feast of Hanukkah

2. What lesson did Jesus teach the apostles by washing their feet?

A. They must obey the command about washing feet in the Law of Moses.
B. They must follow sanitary practices in order to maintain good health.
C. They must serve one another in humility as He served them.
D. They must never again forget to hire a servant when celebrating the Passover.

3. What did Jesus mean when He said to Judas, "What you plan to do, do quickly"?

A. Jesus meant that Judas should go ahead and leave to carry put his plan of betrayal.
B. Jesus meant that Judas should repent of his plan of betrayal.
C. Jesus meant that Judas should give something to the poor.
D. Jesus meant that Judas should buy the things they would need for the festival day.

4. What kind of bread did Jesus use when He instituted the Eucharist?

A. leavened bread
B. unleavened bread
C. rye bread
D. yeast bread

5. When Jesus said to the apostles at the first Eucharist, "Do this in remembrance of Me," what provision was He making for the Church?

A. By these words He explained that the Eucharist they would celebrate was only a memorial service and nothing more.
B. By these words He told them that the Eucharist they would celebrate is only a symbol and nothing more.
C. By these words He told them that the Eucharist they would celebrate is not a sacrament, but only a communion service.
D. By these words He gave to them and to their successors, the priests of the Catholic Church, the power to change bread and wine into His Body and Blood.

6. What was the "new commandment" that Jesus gave His disciples the same night He instituted the Eucharist?

A. He commanded us to love those who love us, but not those who don't love us.
B. He commanded us to love one another as He has loved us.
C. He commanded us to love others the best we can.
D. He commanded us to love one another by being nice to one another.

7. Who was the "Advocate" that Jesus promised God the Father would send to us?

A. the archangel Michael
B. the Blessed Virgin Mary
C. the Holy Spirit
D. the Messiah

8. According to Jesus, how do we know if we are His friends?

A. We are His friends if we make requests to Him in prayer.
B. We are His friends if we talk about Him often.
C. We are His friends if we memorize what He has said.
D. We are His friends if we do what He commands us to do.

9. How did God the Father help Jesus as He was praying in agony in the garden?

A. He sent an angel from heaven to Him, to strengthen Him.
B. He spoke encouraging words from heaven as He had done before.
C. He told Jesus that He didn't have to die if He was too afraid.
D. He woke the apostles so they would pray with Jesus in His agony.

10. How did the soldiers and servants know which man was Jesus when they came searching for Him in the garden?

A. Judas pointed at Jesus and told the soldiers and servants who He was.
B. Judas told the soldiers and servants what kind of clothes Jesus was wearing.
C. Judas kissed Jesus to show the soldiers and servants which man to seize.
D. Judas ordered Jesus to identify Himself to the soldiers and servants.

CHAPTER 15
Christ Before His Accusers

Textbook pages: 185–195
Perfect score: 100

Your Score: _____

Matching

Directions: In each blank beside a phrase, write the letter of the term that is described by that phrase. You may match more than one description to a single term. Each item is worth 4 points. 40 possible points.

A. Annas
B. Herod Antipas
C. praetorium
D. Barabbas
E. Pontius Pilate
F. Gabbatha
G. Sanhedrin
H. Judas
I. Peter

_____ 1. the palace of the Roman governor

_____ 2. arrested for causing a riot that led to a murder

_____ 3. his wife wanted him to have nothing to do with Jesus

_____ 4. the square where the Roman governor's judgment seat was placed

_____ 5. the father-in-law of Caiaphas, the high priest

_____ 6. the ruler of Galilee

_____ 7. the Roman governor

_____ 8. denied Jesus three times

_____ 9. committed suicide

_____ 10. assembled to sit in judgment on Jesus

Multiple Choice

Directions: For each numbered item, circle the letter beside the choice (A, B, C, or D) that best answers the question or completes the statement. Circle only one choice per item. Each correct answer is worth 6 points. 60 possible points.

1. Why did the religious leaders follow whatever advice Annas gave them?

A. Annas had shown himself to be a wise and holy man.
B. They had no one other than Annas who could give them good advice.
C. Annas was secretly plotting an overthrow of the Roman rulers in their country.
D. Even though the Roman governor had deposed him, they continued to view Annas as the real high priest.

2. How did Jesus respond when Annas began to question Him about His teaching?

A. Jesus said that Annas had no reason to question Him about His teaching, because He had always taught openly in the synagogue and in the Temple.
B. Jesus said that His teaching was a secret revealed only to His disciples, so He couldn't reveal it to Annas.
C. Jesus refused to speak to Annas at all because he was a wicked man.
D. Jesus told Annas to repent and become one of His disciples.

3. What took place with Peter in the courtyard at the palace of the high priest?

A. He defended Jesus against the accusations of the high priest's servants.
B. He told stories to pass the time with the others who were gathered there.
C. He lied when someone claimed that he was one of Jesus' disciples.
D. He preached the gospel to those who were gathered there.

4. What did Jesus say that made the high priest declare He had blasphemed?

A. Jesus declared that the high priest and the council were sinners to be judged by God.
B. Jesus spoke of Himself as the Son of Man who would one day come in the clouds of heaven.
C. Jesus claimed that He would destroy the Temple at God's command.
D. Jesus announced that all people were sons and daughters of God.

5. In Jewish law, what was the punishment for blasphemy?

A. death
B. imprisonment
C. forty lashes
D. a fine of a thousand shekels

6. If Jewish law permitted the Sanhedrin to declare someone guilty of a crime punishable by death, why couldn't they order his execution?

A. The Romans forbade the Jews to practice any of the Law of Moses.
B. The order for execution took a unanimous vote of the Sanhedrin, and that rarely happened.
C. It was too expensive to hire executioners to carry put the sentence.
D. The Romans reserved to their governor the power to execute criminals.

7. What did the chief priests do with the money that Judas gave back to them?

A. They placed in in the Temple treasury.
B. They kept it for themselves.
C. They gave it to the poor.
D. They bought a potter's field, the burying place for strangers.

8. Why did Pilate ask Jesus, "Are You the king of the Jews?"

A. If Jesus truly was a Jewish king, He could not be executed.
B. If Jesus truly was a Jewish king, Pilate wanted to honor Him.
C. If Jesus truly was claiming to be a Jewish king, He could be accused of treason against Rome.
D. If Jesus truly was claiming to be a Jewish king, His case would have to be tried in Rome.

9. Why was Herod glad to see Jesus?

A. Herod was curious about Jesus.
B. Herod wanted to see Jesus work a miracle.
C. Herod wanted to make sure that Jesus wasn't really John the Baptist, returned from the dead.
D. All of the above.

10. Why did the Roman soldiers place a purple cloak and a crown of thorns on Jesus, and a reed in His right hand?

A. These were the only items they had on hand with which to torment Him.
B. They did this to all the prisoners who were to be crucified.
C. These were mock royal garments for "the King of the Jews."
D. They were taking revenge on Jesus for rebuking them.

CHAPTER 16
Jesus Is Crucified, Dies, and Is Buried

Textbook pages: 197–206
Perfect score: 100

Your Score: _____

Matching

Directions: In each blank beside a phrase, write the letter of the term that is described by that phrase. Each item is worth 4 points. 40 possible points.

A. Golgotha
B. Simon of Cyrene
C. Nicodemus
D. Calvary
E. Mary, the mother of Jesus; John; and Mary Magdalene
F. Joseph of Arimathea
G. centurion
H. Eli, Eli, lama sabachthani
I. myrrh
J. Veronica

_____ 1. commander of a hundred soldiers

_____ 2. deadened pain when mixed with wine

_____ 3. name from the Latin word for "skull"

_____ 4. means, "My God, my God, why have You abandoned Me?"

_____ 5. offered Jesus a towel to wipe away the blood and filth from His face

_____ 6. stood at the foot of the Cross

_____ 7. means "place of the skull"

_____ 8. brought a mixture of myrrh and aloes for Jesus' burial

_____ 9. asked Pilate for the body of Jesus

_____ 10. was forced to carry the cross behind Jesus

Multiple Choice

Directions: For each numbered item, circle the letter beside the choice (A, B, C, or D) that best answers the question or completes the statement. Circle only one choice per item. Each correct answer is worth 6 points. 60 possible points.

1. Which of the following was the Roman way of putting criminals to death?

A. hanging
B. crucifixion
C. burning
D. stoning

2. Why didn't Jesus accept the drink offered to Him to deaden His pain?

A. He refused it because He didn't like the taste of it.
B. He was unconscious and unable to drink it.
C. He refused it because He thought the soldiers were trying to poison Him.
D. He wanted to drink to the last drop the cup of suffering that His Father had given Him.

3. What was written on the title nailed to Jesus' cross?

A. "Jesus Christ, Savior of the World"
B. "Jesus of Nazareth, King of the Jews"
C. "Jesus of Nazareth, Messiah of the Jews"
D. "Jesus Christ, Lord of the World"

4. Which languages were used to write the title nailed to Jesus' cross?

A. Latin, Greek, and Aramaic
B. Latin, Greek, and Egyptian
C. Latin, Roman, and Greek
D. Aramaic, Latin, and Hebrew

5. What were Jesus' first recorded words while hanging on the Cross?

A. "Father, forgive them, for they don't know what they're doing."
B. "Father, never forget this evil that they have done to Me!"
C. "My people will be judged for their wickedness!"
D. "Why have My disciples abandoned Me?"

6. Why did the soldiers at the Cross cast lots for Jesus' tunic?

A. They were bored and wanted a game to keep them entertained.
B. Soldiers always cast lots for the clothes of crucified prisoners.
C. The tunic had been woven in one piece, so dividing it would have destroyed it.
D. Casting lots kept their minds off the terrible deed they were committing.

7. What did the robbers who were crucified alongside Jesus have to say to Him?

A. They both cursed and mocked Jesus.
B. They both begged Jesus to forgive them.
C. One of them cursed Jesus, but the other asked Him for mercy.
D. They asked Jesus to work a miracle to save them from death.

8. When Jesus said to John from His cross, "There is your mother," what did He mean?

A. Jesus was revealing that Mary had actually adopted John when he was an infant.
B. Jesus was saying that the Church would now become John's mother.
C. John's mother was standing nearby, and Jesus wanted to recognize her.
D. Jesus was giving to John and to all people His greatest treasure on earth, His mother.

9. How did it happen that the veil of the Temple was torn in two?

A. It was torn in two, from the bottom to the top, by Roman soldiers at the command of Pilate.
B. It was torn in two, from the top to the bottom, by the hand of God Himself.
C. It was torn in two by the high priest, to show his grief over Jesus' crucifixion.
D. It was torn in two by Jesus' disciples to protest His murder.

10. Why did the chief priests and Pharisees want Pilate to have the tomb of Jesus guarded?

A. They feared that His disciples might steal away His body and tell the people He had risen from the dead.
B. They feared that the crowds who had hailed Him when He entered Jerusalem might demand that His body be moved to a more lavish tomb.
C. They feared that wild dogs might try to enter the tomb.
D. They feared that Jesus' enemies might come to disturb His body.

CHAPTER 17
The Proof of Christ's Divinity

Textbook pages: 207–219
Perfect score: 100

Your Score: _____

Matching

Directions: In each blank beside a phrase, write the letter of the term that is described by that phrase. Each item is worth 4 points. 40 possible points.

A. Mary Magdalene and Mary, the mother of James and Salome
B. Cleopas
C. Thomas
D. Peter and John
E. Matthias
F. Peter
G. Mary Magdalene
H. Barsabbas
I. Bethany
J. Emmaus

_____ 1. the first disciples of Jesus to find out His tomb was empty

_____ 2. a town about seven miles from Jerusalem

_____ 3. chosen to take the place of Judas

_____ 4. another candidate to replace Judas

_____ 5. a disciple who walked along the road with Jesus without recognizing Him

_____ 6. came to the tomb of Jesus with spices to anoint His body

_____ 7. where the apostles gathered for Jesus' ascension into heaven

_____ 8. could not believe Jesus had been raised from the dead unless he touched His wounds

_____ 9. it was prophesied that he would one day die for Jesus' sake

_____ 10. spoke to Jesus at the tomb without at first realizing who He was

Multiple Choice

Directions: For each numbered item, circle the letter beside the choice (A, B, C, or D) that best answers the question or completes the statement. Circle only one choice per item. Each correct answer is worth 6 points. 60 possible points.

1. Why did the soldiers leave the tomb unguarded on Sunday morning?

A. They went to look for breakfast and planned to return afterward.
B. Pilate ordered them to return to his palace after the Sabbath was over.
C. They went to the high priest to demand more money for standing guard.
D. They saw a dazzling angel roll the stone away from the tomb, so they fled in terror.

2. How did the three women, when they returned to the tomb, find out that Jesus had risen from the dead?

A. One of the guards had returned and told them what had happened.
B. Jesus Himself was waiting for them there and told them what had happened.
C. What appeared to be a young man seated in the tomb told them Jesus had risen.
D. The gardener who took care of the tomb told them Jesus had risen.

3. How did Peter and John come to believe that Jesus was risen from the dead?

A. When they went to the tomb, they found it empty except for Jesus' grave clothes.
B. Mary Magdalene told them that Jesus had risen.
C. The women told them that they themselves had seen Jesus.
D. All of the above.

4. How did the Sanhedrin respond to the news that the tomb was empty and the guards had run away?

A. They had no choice but to believe that Jesus had risen.
B. They bribed the guards to tell everyone that Jesus' disciples had stolen His body.
C. They demanded that Pilate have the guards executed for leaving their post.
D. They had the disciples arrested and imprisoned before they could tell others what had happened.

5. When did the disciples who walked to Emmaus recognize that the stranger they had met was actually Jesus?

A. They recognized Him when He began teaching them how he fulfilled the prophecies of Scripture.
B. They recognized Him when He called them each by name.
C. They recognized Him when He celebrated the Eucharist with them.
D. They didn't recognize Him until after He had gone.

6. When Jesus appeared to the disciples in the upper room, how did He convince them that He wasn't a ghost?

A. He showed them His wounds in His hands and feet.
B. He ate a piece of broiled fish and a honeycomb.
C. He told them He wasn't a ghost.
D. All of the above.

7. What happened to the apostles when Jesus breathed on them and said, "Receive the Holy Spirit"?

A. The apostles were given the authority to forgive sins on His behalf.
B. At that moment the Holy Spirit descended on the apostles like tongues of fire and a mighty wind.
C. The apostles were given the authority to preach the gospel.
D. The apostles had all their sins forgiven, and they never sinned again.

8. Why did Jesus say to Peter, "Feed my sheep"?

A. Jesus was saying that He Himself would no longer be the Good Shepherd.
B. Jesus was giving Peter the primary responsibility to care for His flock.
C. Jesus was asking Peter to take care of Mary, His mother.
D. Jesus was telling Peter that he would be the only pastor in the Church.

9. What did the two angels tell the apostles after Jesus ascended into heaven?

A. The angels said that Jesus had gone to heaven and would never return to earth.
B. The angels said that Jesus would return to earth in forty days.
C. The angels said that Jesus would return to earth, but only in the hearts of His disciples.
D. The angels said that Jesus would come back to earth in the same way He had gone into heaven.

10. How did the eleven apostles discern who should take the place of Judas?

A. They voted for candidates from among the other disciples, and the majority candidate was made an apostle.
B. They voted for candidates from among the other disciples, and the decision was unanimous.
C. They selected two men who had long been with them, then cast lots so that God could show them which man He had chosen.
D. When a dove came and rested on the head of one of the disciples, they knew the Holy Spirit had chosen him.

PART FOUR
How the Apostles Became the Foundation of the Church

CHAPTER 18
The Growth of the Early Church

Textbook pages: 221–230
Perfect score: 100

Your Score: _____

Matching

Directions: In each blank beside a phrase, write the letter of the term that is described by that phrase. You may match more than one description to a single term. Each item is worth 4 points. 40 possible points.

A. Joel
B. Peter and John
C. Hellenists
D. the Holy Spirit

E. Stephen and Nicolaus
F. Hebrews
G. Gamaliel
H. Peter

_____ 1. the sick were healed just by having his shadow fall on them

_____ 2. Pharisee and teacher of the Law respected by all the people

_____ 3. Jewish converts who spoke Aramaic

_____ 4. Old Testament prophet who predicted that God would pour out His Spirit on all people

_____ 5. arrested twice for preaching about Jesus

_____ 6. among the first deacons of the Church

_____ 7. scourged for preaching the gospel

_____ 8. healed a lame man at the Temple

_____ 9. came upon the apostles on Pentecost

_____ 10. Jewish converts who spoke Greek

Multiple Choice

Directions: For each numbered item, circle the letter beside the choice (A, B, C, or D) that best answers the question or completes the statement. Circle only one choice per item. Each correct answer is worth 6 points. 60 possible points.

1. What took place while the disciples were gathered in an upper room, united in prayer?

A. A sound came from heaven, like a mighty wind, and shook the whole house.
B. Tongues of fire appeared and settled on each of them.
C. They began to speak in foreign languages that they had never learned.
D. All of the above.

2. What was the response of the crowds to Peter's Pentecost sermon?

A. They became furious and tried to stone him to death.
B. About three thousand people were converted and baptized.
C. Most were too busy to pay much attention, so they ignored him.
D. They called him a liar for saying that Jesus was alive again.

3. How did the first Christians worship?

A. They gathered to pray.
B. They listened to the teaching of the apostles.
C. They celebrated the Eucharist.
D. All of the above.

4. What was it about the early Christians that deeply impressed those around them?

A. They never committed a sin.
B. They read their Bibles every day.
C. They showed a joyful, generous charity toward others.
D. They never talked about their faith, but just lived good lives.

5. What surprise did the beggar at the Beautiful Gate receive from the apostles?

A. He thought they would give him alms, but instead, they healed his disability.
B. He thought they would give him copper coins, but instead, they gave him silver and gold.
C. He thought they would give him alms, but instead, they refused to give him anything.
D. He thought they would give him alms, but instead, they just preached to him.

6. Why were the chief priests amazed at Peter and John's boldness in preaching?

A. People had told them that the two apostles were shy and afraid to speak in public.
B. They knew that the two apostles were fishermen without the kind of training that religious teachers were expected to have.
C. They had expected Jesus' followers to give up their faith in Him after He died.

D. They had offered the two apostles thirty pieces of silver if they would stop preaching.

7. How did Peter and John escape from prison?

A. An angel opened the doors of the prison and let them out.
B. They bribed the prison guards to let them escape.
C. They slipped quietly past the guards while they were sleeping.
D. Some of the other disciples helped them escape through a window.

8. What was Gamaliel's advice to the Sanhedrin?

A. He told them that the apostles should be executed immediately.
B. He told them that the apostles were sent by God, so the members of the Sanhedrin should become Jesus' disciples.
C. He told them to leave the apostles alone, because God might be working through them.
D. He told them that the apostles were foolish fishermen and should be put in prison.

9. Why were the first deacons ordained in the Church?

A. The apostles needed men to focus on practical responsibilities, so they themselves could focus on teaching, providing the sacraments, and governing the Church.
B. The apostles couldn't find enough men to ordain as priests, so they decided to ordain deacons.
C. All the new disciples got together and demanded that the apostles ordain deacons.
D. They followed the example of the Jewish leaders in the Temple, who had ordained deacons.

10. How did the apostles ordain the first deacons?

A. The apostles had all the disciples stand in line to pray for the men and lay hands on them.
B. The apostles prayed for the men and laid hands on them.
C. The apostles took the men to the Temple priests to ordain them.
D. All of the above.

CHAPTER 19
The Seed of God Is Scattered

Textbook pages: 231–243
Perfect score: 100

Your Score: _____

Matching

Directions: In each blank beside a phrase, write the letter of the term that is described by that phrase. You may match more than one description to a single term. Each item is worth 3 points. 45 possible points.

A. Saul   C. Simon   E. Cornelius   G. Peter   I. Herod

B. Aeneas   D. Philip   F. Stephen   H. presbyter   J. Tabitha

_____ 1. the first Christian martyr

_____ 2. offered the apostles money for the gift of bestowing the Holy Spirit

_____ 3. preached the gospel to an Ethiopian official

_____ 4. means "gazelle"

_____ 5. stood watching, with approval, as a deacon was stoned to death

_____ 6. raised from the dead through Peter's prayer

_____ 7. a sorcerer who called himself "the Power of God"

_____ 8. Roman centurion who believed in the one true God

_____ 9. a paralytic who was healed through Peter's prayer

_____ 10. deacon who preached and worked miracles in Samaria

_____ 11. a priest (literally, "elder")

_____ 12. had James killed with a sword

_____ 13. had a vision about unclean animals

_____ 14. judged by God and died from parasites

_____ 15. convert who preached the gospel to the Gentiles

Multiple Choice

Directions: For each numbered item, circle the letter beside the choice (A, B, C, or D) that best answers the question or completes the statement. Circle only one choice per item. Each correct answer is worth 5 points. 55 possible points.

1. What did Stephen pray as he was being stoned to death for His faith in Christ?

A. "Lord, be my judge!"
B. "Lord, don't forget what my persecutors have done."
C. "Lord, save me from my enemies!"
D. "Lord, don't hold this sin against them."

2. Why did Peter say to the sorcerer, "May your silver perish with you"?

A. The sorcerer was trying to bribe Peter to become a magician.
B. Peter knew the sorcerer was a wealthy man who didn't help the poor.
C. The sorcerer thought the gift of God could be bought with money.
D. The sorcerer cheated people out of their money by pretending to work magic.

3. Why did Philip run up to the Ethiopian's chariot and greet him?

A. Philip was tired of walking and hoped to get a ride in the chariot.
B. Philip's curiosity was aroused by seeing an African in splendid attire.
C. The Holy Spirit had told him to go talk to the Ethiopian.
D. Philip was hungry and hoped the Ethiopian would share his food.

4. Why did the Ethiopian welcome Philip into his chariot?

A. The Ethiopian was reading the Book of Isaiah and needed help to understand it.
B. The Ethiopian was bored and wanted to talk with someone.
C. The Ethiopian hoped to kidnap Philip and bring him back to Africa.
D. The Ethiopian was a spy for the Sanhedrin.

5. What happened after Philip baptized the Ethiopian?

A. The Ethiopian returned with Philip to Jerusalem and became one of the apostles.
B. When they came up out of the water, the Spirit of the Lord took Philip away.
C. The Ethiopian's queen threatened him with death if he didn't give up his new faith.
D. The Ethiopian translated the Scriptures into his native language.

6. Why did many people come to believe in Jesus in the city of Joppa?

A. Jesus had spent much time in Joppa during His years of ministry.
B. Mary Magdalene had relatives in Joppa who had heard from her about Jesus' resurrection.
C. Peter raised a woman from the dead in that city.
D. There were no scribes or Pharisees in that city.

7. How did God prepare Peter for his meeting with Cornelius?

A. He sent an angel announcing that Cornelius was on his way.
B. He arranged for Peter to meet some of Cornelius' relatives.
C. He gave Peter the gift of speaking in tongues so that he could converse with Cornelius in Latin, his native language.
D. He sent Peter a vision showing him that there should be no barriers between the Jews and the Gentiles in Christ.

8. How did Peter and the Jewish believers with him in Joppa know that the Holy Spirit had come on the Gentiles who were listening to him speak?

A. The Gentiles told them that they could feel the Holy Spirit in their hearts.
B. They heard the Gentiles speaking in tongues and praising God, just as the Jewish believers had done at Pentecost.
C. The Gentiles began working miracles.
D. The Gentiles were weeping with great joy.

9. Where were the disciples first called "Christians"?

A. Jerusalem
B. Joppa
C. Antioch
D. Caesaria

10. What did the believers gathered to pray for Peter's release from prison say when the maid told them he was at the door?

A. They believed her immediately and all ran to the door to greet Peter.
B. They said it was just Peter's guardian angel at the door.
C. They said she was crazy, because Peter was in prison.
D. Both B and C above.

11. How did the apostles provide for the Church's leadership after their death?

A. They consecrated bishops who would be their successors and carry on their work.
B. They wrote all the books of the New Testament as a guide for Church leaders.
C. Both A and B above.
D. None of the above.

CHAPTER 20
Paul's Conversion and Early Ministry

Textbook pages: 245–252
Perfect score: 100

Your Score: _____

Matching

Directions: In each blank beside a phrase, write the letter of the term that is described by that phrase. You may match more than one description to a single term. Each item is worth 4 points. 40 possible points.

A. Tarsus
B. Barnabas
C. Zeus
D. Paul
E. Hermes
F. Ananias
G. Damascus
H. Cyprus

_____ 1. Saul's Latin name

_____ 2. an island in the Mediterranean Sea

_____ 3. Barnabas was mistaken for this Greek god

_____ 4. a great city of Syria

_____ 5. sent to Saul so Saul could regain his sight

_____ 6. a missionary companion of Paul

_____ 7. Saul's hometown

_____ 8. influential in the Church at Jerusalem because of his preaching and holiness

_____ 9. Paul was mistaken for this Greek god

_____ 10. Saul's sponsor in Jerusalem

Multiple Choice

Directions: For each numbered item, circle the letter beside the choice (A, B, C, or D) that best answers the question or completes the statement. Circle only one choice per item. Each correct answer is worth 6 points. 60 possible points.

1. Why was Saul on his way to Damascus?

A. He was born in Damascus and wanted to visit family members there.
B. He opposed the Christians, so he wanted to search for them in Damascus and bring them back in chains to Jerusalem.
C. He wanted to become a Christian, and he had heard that the apostles were preaching in Damascus.
D. He was curious about what Christians believed, and he knew he could find Christians in Damascus.

2. How was Saul converted to the Christian faith?

A. Peter preached to him and he repented.
B. Reading the Scriptures convinced him that Jesus was the Messiah.
C. He was inspired by the deaths of Christian martyrs.
D. Jesus came to him in a blinding light.

3. Why was Ananias reluctant to pray for Saul?

A. Saul had asked him to pray for a miracle, and Ananias didn't know whether God would answer his prayer.
B. Saul was always bothering Ananias with prayer requests.
C. Ananias wanted Saul to pray for him instead.
D. Saul had a reputation for persecuting Christians.

4. How did Saul spend his time while he was waiting for God's direction and help?

A. Saul spent the time in prayer and fasting.
B. Saul spent the time reading Scripture.
C. Saul spent the time relaxing and getting rest.
D. All of the above.

5. Once Saul became a Christian, how was he able to convince many Jewish people that Jesus was the promised Messiah?

A. His personal example of patience and gentleness won them over.
B. As a Pharisee who had trained under one of the great rabbis of his time, Saul knew the Scriptures well.
C. Both A and B above.
D. None of the above.

6. How did Saul get past the assassins in Damascus who intended to kill him?

A. He went through a secret tunnel that led outside the city.
B. He passed by them in a crafty disguise.
C. He left secretly in the middle of the night under the cover of darkness.
D. His friends lowered him down outside the city wall in a great basket.

7. What were the Christian leaders in Antioch doing when the Holy Spirit spoke to them about which missionaries to send out?

A. They were sleeping, and the Holy Spirit spoke to them in a dream.
B. They were debating Scripture when the Holy Spirit spoke to them.
C. They were praying and fasting to seek God's will.
D. They were casting lots to see which missionaries should be sent.

8. How did the opponents of the Christians treat Paul after he preached in Lystra?

A. They spent the night debating him in the synagogue.
B. They bound him and placed him on a ship headed back to Antioch.
C. They stoned him and left him for dead.
D. They were finally converted by his preaching and miracles.

9. Why did Paul and Barnabas usually begin their mission in a city by preaching in the local Jewish synagogue?

A. They spoke only Hebrew and Aramaic, and they knew that the Jewish people in the synagogues would understand these languages.
B. They knew the Gentiles would throw them out of town if they began preaching in the city square.
C. They expected most of the Jews in the synagogue to be converted right away at their preaching.
D. They wanted the local Jewish population to have the chance to believe first.

10. How did the apostles decide whether the Gentile Christians had to observe all the Law of Moses?

A. The apostles sent all the believers home to read the Scriptures and decide the matter for themselves.
B. The apostles met together in a council, and the Holy Spirit guided them to declare God's will in the matter.
C. The whole community of disciples took a vote, and the majority ruled.
D. The apostles said that it didn't really matter, as long as everyone loved one another.

CHAPTER 21
Paul Takes the Gospel to Europe

Textbook pages: 253–261
Perfect score: 100

Your Score: _____

Matching

Directions: In each blank beside a phrase, write the letter of the term that is described by that phrase. You may match more than one description to a single term. Each item is worth 4 points. 40 possible points.

A. John Mark
B. Macedonia
C. Areopagus
D. Timothy
E. Aquila and Priscilla
F. Thessalonica
G. Silas
H. Philippi
I. Corinth
J. Lydia

_____ 1. companion of Paul whose father was a Gentile but whose mother was a Jewish Christian

_____ 2. the leading city of Macedonia and a Roman colony

_____ 3. a wealthy merchant who sold cloth for royal courts

_____ 4. a land north of Greece

_____ 5. city where the mob accused the Christians of acting against the decrees of Caesar

_____ 6. a young disciple who accompanied Barnabas

_____ 7. tentmakers in whose home Paul stayed

_____ 8. city where the leader of the synagogue and his household all became Christians

_____ 9. where people gathered daily in Athens to hear the latest news and to debate ideas

_____ 10. a prophet and teacher chosen to bring the Jerusalem council's message to Antioch

Multiple Choice

Directions: For each numbered item, circle the letter beside the choice (A, B, C, or D) that best answers the question or completes the statement. Circle only one choice per item. Each correct answer is worth 6 points. 60 possible points.

1. On his second missionary journey, why did Paul change his plans to preach in several more cities of Asia Minor?

A. Paul heard that his enemies in Asia Minor were seeking to kill him.
B. The Holy Spirit gave Paul a vision one night to direct him to Macedonia instead.
C. Paul found it difficult to speak in the language of Asia Minor.
D. The journey to Asia Minor was difficult, and winter was approaching.

2. Paul's first missionary effort on the continent of Europe was in:

A. Philippi
B. Corinth
C. Thessalonica
D. Antioch

3. Why did some Jewish residents of Philippi gather by the riverside for prayer rather than in the synagogue?

A. They were persecuted by the Gentiles and had to meet in secret.
B. They preferred to worship outdoors rather than in the synagogue.
C. The people of the synagogue had argued over the interpretation of Scripture, so one group left and met by the riverside instead.
D. They had no synagogue in which to meet.

4. Why did the apostles want the slave girl to stop telling everyone that they were "servants of the Most High God"?

A. She was causing a commotion.
B. People probably thought she was hired to promote the missionaries.
C. She was known to be a demon-possessed fortuneteller.
D. All of the above.

5. Why did the girl's masters seize Paul and Silas after Paul cast the demon out of her?

A. They realized that their hope of profit from her fortunetelling had fled along with the demon.
B. They wanted Paul and Silas to show them how to cast out demons.
C. They intended to make Paul and Silas their slaves as well.
D. They didn't like the message that Paul and Silas were preaching about Jesus.

6. How did Paul and Silas spend the evening hours in prison in Philippi?

A. They kept demanding that the guards release them.
B. They asked the disciples in Philippi to bring them bandages and ointment for their wounds.
C. They prayed and sang hymns, joyful that they had been considered worthy to suffer for Jesus.
D. They prayed quietly so as not to disturb the other prisoners.

7. What happened to Paul and Silas at midnight in the prison in Philippi?

A. An earthquake made the prison doors fly open and their chains fall off, but they refused to escape.
B. An earthquake freed them from the prison, and they escaped into hiding.
C. An angel appeared and led them to freedom and safety.
D. The prison guard thought they had escaped, so he killed himself.

8. Why did so many of the Athenians reject Paul's message?

A. They were more interested in playing with new ideas than in taking them seriously.
B. The Greeks tended to look down on the human body as a prison to be escaped at death, so they were scandalized by the notion of a resurrection.
C. Both A and B above.
D. None of the above.

9. What approach to preaching did Paul employ in the Areopagus?

A. He told the Greeks that they knew nothing about the true God.
B. He started by noting certain pagan beliefs and practices that pointed to the truth about God.
C. He explained to them how Jesus was the Messiah that God had promised in the Scriptures.
D. He said that the Jewish God was really just the Greek god Zeus by another name.

10. What was the result of Paul's preaching in Corinth?

A. The entire city was converted and became Christians.
B. Paul and his fellow missionaries were quickly run out of town.
C. The city rulers threw Paul in prison and kept him there for months.
D. Despite opposition, the missionaries had great success, so that a thriving church was established there.

CHAPTER 22
Paul's Last Missionary Journey

Textbook pages: 263–268
Perfect score: 100

Your Score: _____

Matching

Directions: In each blank beside a phrase, write the letter of the term that is described by that phrase. Each item is worth 4 points. 20 possible points.

A. Demetrius
B. Sceva
C. Ephesus
D. Miletus
E. Eutychus

_____ 1. a Jewish high priest with seven sons

_____ 2. fell out of a third-story window to his death

_____ 3. where Paul gave a farewell address to the priests of Ephesus

_____ 4. a pagan silversmith at Ephesus

_____ 5. a great center of worship for the Greek goddess Artemis

Multiple Choice

Directions: For each numbered item, circle the letter beside the choice (A, B, C, or D) that best answers the question or completes the statement. Circle only one choice per item. Each correct answer is worth 8 points. 80 possible points.

1. How many of Paul's missionary journeys are recorded in Scripture?

A. one
B. two
C. three
D. five

2. How did Paul know that the Christian formation of the disciples he found in Ephesus was quite limited?

A. They didn't know about the Holy Spirit.
B. They had not yet received Christian baptism.
C. Both A and B above.
D. None of the above.

3. Why was the baptism of John not sufficient for the disciples at Ephesus?

A. The disciples had no record of their baptisms.
B. John's baptism had prepared the way for Jesus, but it wasn't the same as Christian baptism, which they still needed to receive.
C. In John's baptism, water was sprinkled, not poured.
D. All the disciples had to receive two baptisms: the baptism of John and Christian baptism.

4. Why did the people in Ephesus press handkerchiefs and aprons to Paul's body?

A. It was winter time, and they wanted to keep him warm.
B. It was a pagan ritual that had been practiced for generations.
C. They knew they could sell these items for a high price.
D. When they carried these items away to lay on the sick and demon-possessed, the sick were healed and the demons were cast out.

5. What happened when seven exorcists tried to cast demons out of a man in Jesus' name, even though they weren't Christians?

A. The possessed man simply ignored them.
B. The possessed man leapt at them and violently overpowered all seven of them at once.
C. The demons had to flee because they feared the name of Jesus.
D. The exorcism worked, so the seven men became Christians.

6. How did the sorcerers who became Christians demonstrate that they would no longer practice sorcery?

A. They solemnly promised Paul that they would never practice sorcery again.
B. They denounced sorcery in the words of the rite of Baptism.
C. They collected their books of magic and burned them publicly.
D. They went back to their sorcerer friends and preached the gospel to them.

7. Why were the silversmiths in Ephesus so angry at Paul?

A. The people were giving their silver coins to Paul instead of to the silversmiths.
B. The silversmiths sold little silver shrines of the goddess Artemis, and when people became Christians, they no longer bought the shrines.
C. Paul was teaching that Artemis was just another name for Jesus' mother, Mary.
D. The Christians were throwing away the necklaces and jewelry that the silversmiths had made.

8. How did a young Christian in Troas fall out of a third-story window to his death?

A. He was sitting in the window, listening to Paul preach, and fell asleep.
B. He was fleeing from Roman soldiers who were trying to arrest him.
C. He was trying to save a child from falling out of the window.
D. He had drunk too much wine and was unsteady.

9. Why did Paul want to return to Jerusalem, even though he knew it would be dangerous for him to go there?

A. Paul had family members in Jerusalem, and he hadn't seen them in many years.
B. Paul was seriously ill, and if he was going to die, he wanted to die in Jerusalem.
C. Paul was convinced that God wanted him to return to Jerusalem.
D. Paul hoped to convert the chief priests at the Temple in Jerusalem.

10. In his farewell address to the priests, what did Paul say would happen in the future?

A. The persecution of the Church would soon end, and Christians everywhere would enjoy peace.
B. Paul himself would live a long and fruitful life into old age, bringing many more people to Christ.
C. One day, some of the priests among them would spread false teaching and draw the disciples away from God.
D. One day, the entire Roman Empire would become Christian.

CHAPTER 23
Paul in Jerusalem and Rome

Textbook pages: 269–280
Perfect score: 100

Your Score: _____

Matching

Directions: In each blank beside a phrase, write the letter of the term that is described by that phrase. Each item is worth 4 points. 40 possible points.

A. Luke
B. Agrippa
C. John
D. Julius
E. Malta
F. Nero
G. heresies
H. Agabus
I. apostolic succession
J. epistles

_____ 1. false religious teachings

_____ 2. a man who prophesied Paul's future

_____ 3. letters written by the apostles to the early Christians

_____ 4. Roman emperor who had Paul beheaded for being a Christian

_____ 5. an unbroken chain of bishops stretching back to the time of Our Lord

_____ 6. physician who wrote the Book of Acts

_____ 7. son of Herod

_____ 8. wrote the Book of Revelation

_____ 9. island where Paul was shipwrecked

_____ 10. centurion assigned to guard Paul on his voyage to Rome

Multiple Choice

Directions: For each numbered item, circle the letter beside the choice (A, B, C, or D) that best answers the question or completes the statement. Circle only one choice per item. Each correct answer is worth 6 points. 60 possible points.

1. Why did Paul's companions beg him not to go to Jerusalem?

A. They couldn't go with him, and they didn't want him to leave them behind.
B. Paul was seriously ill, and they thought he might die if he tried to travel so far.
C. A prophet had predicted that in Jerusalem, Paul would be bound and handed over to the Gentiles.
D. Paul still had unfinished work to do in the cities of Asia Minor.

2. How was Paul saved from being murdered by a mob in Jerusalem?

A. An angel appeared and sent the mob fleeing in terror.
B. The Roman tribune and his soldiers stopped the mob from assaulting him.
C. The Christians in Jerusalem chased the mob away with swords.
D. The leader of the mob was instantly converted, and he commanded the others to stop beating Paul.

3. How did Paul avoid being taken to the barracks, scourged, and interrogated with torture by the Roman soldiers?

A. Paul was spirited away through the crowd by the disciples.
B. Paul bribed the tribune to let him go.
C. Paul assured the tribune that he would be happy to answer all his questions.
D. Paul told the tribune that he was a Roman citizen, so it would be illegal to mistreat him that way.

4. What was Paul's strategy to keep the Sanhedrin from condemning him?

A. Paul provoked an argument between the Pharisees and Sadducees so that they couldn't agree on a verdict.
B. Paul told the Sanhedrin that he was a Pharisee, not a Christian.
C. Each day when they assembled, Paul pretended to be too ill to appear before the council.
D. Paul persuaded the Roman tribune to dismiss the council meeting.

5. Why did Festus order that Paul be brought to Rome for trial before a Roman court?

A. Paul had appealed his case to Rome, which was his right as a Roman citizen.
B. Festus did not feel competent to judge religious matters.
C. Festus was tired of dealing with Paul and the Sanhedrin.
D. It was expensive for Festus to keep Paul in the local prison for so long.

6. When a terrible storm threatened to sink Paul's ship, how could he promise the crew that their lives would not be lost?

A. In a vision, Paul had seen the ship sail safely to port.
B. An angel had assured Paul that despite a shipwreck, none of them would perish.
C. Paul knew that the ship was well constructed and could survive the storm.
D. The captain of the ship was confident that his crew could handle the storm.

7. Why did the people of Malta think Paul was a god?

A. Paul's face glowed with a mysterious light as he preached.
B. Paul could prophesy the future.
C. Paul walked on water to the shore from the ship.
D. When a poisonous viper bit Paul, he suffered no harm.

8. Which was the only apostle who did not die a martyr's death for his faith in Christ?

A. John
B. Philip
C. Nathaniel
D. Matthew

9. How do the biblical epistles add to our knowledge of Bible history?

A. They provide hints about how the churches were structured, how the apostles ministered, and how the people worshipped.
B. They take us deeper into the minds, the hearts, and even the personalities of their authors.
C. Through them, we gain some sense of the circumstances the apostles encountered among the early Christians.
D. All of the above.

10. What is the main message of the Book of Revelation?

A. The end of the world is coming soon.
B. The Church will be destroyed by the Antichrist.
C. Christians will avoid the great tribulation at the end of the world.
D. No matter how many difficulties the Church may suffer, Jesus is the Lord of history.

Answer Key

INTRODUCTION – Your Time Has Come
Test Book pages 9–12

Multiple Choice
1. D 2. C 3. D 4. A 5. C 6. B 7. B 8. D 9. D 10. A 11. B 12. B
13. D 14. C 15. A

Old Testament or New?
1. NT	2. NT	3. OT	4. NT	5. OT	6. NT
7. OT	8. OT	9. OT	10. OT	11. OT	12. OT
13. NT	14. NT	15. NT	16. OT	17. OT	18. NT
19. OT	20. OT				

PART ONE – How Christ Prepared to Redeem the World

CHAPTER 1 – The World Into Which the Messiah Came
Test Book pages 13–17

Matching
1. E 2. C 3. A 4. D 5. B

Matching: Cities and Provinces of Ancient Palestine
1. D 2. G 3. C 4. A 5. B 6. E 7. F

Matching: Coins of Ancient Palestine
1. B 2. E 3. C 4. D 5. F 6. A

Matching: Religious Life in Ancient Palestine
1. J 2. E 3. L 4. F 5. A 6. H 7. B 8. C 9. I 10. D 11. K 12. G

Multiple Choice
1. C 2. D 3. C 4. A 5. C 6. A 7. D 8. B 9. C 10. A

CHAPTER 2 – The Redeemer Comes to Earth
Test Book pages 19-22

Matching
1. G   2. D   3. F   4. A   5. L   6. B   7. J   8. E   9. C   10. O   11. I   12. N
13. M   14. K   15. H

Multiple Choice
1. C   2. A   3. D   4. B   5. C   6. A   7. C   8. D   9. B   10. C   11. C

PART TWO – How Christ Ministered

CHAPTER 3 – Christ Begins His Public Ministry
Test Book pages 23-26

Matching
1. D   2. B   3. G   4. C   5. F   6. A   7. H   8. E

Matching: The Apostles
1. B   2. D   3. G   4. J   5. I   6. E   7. K   8. A   9. L   10. F   11. H   12. C

Multiple Choice
1. D   2. B   3. A   4. B   5. C   6. A   7. C   8. A   9. A   10. D

CHAPTER 4 – Christ Calls All People to Repentance
Test Book pages 27-29

Matching
1. C   2. D   3. B   4. F   5. A   6. H   7. E   8. G   9. I   10. G

Multiple Choice
1. C   2. A   3. B   4. A   5. C   6. C   7. D   8. A   9. B   10. D

CHAPTER 5 – Christ, the Great Teacher
Test Book pages 31–34

Matching
1. C   2. D   3. E   4. B   5. A

Multiple Choice
1. B   2. D   3. C   4. D   5. C   6. A   7. D   8. C   9. A   10. C   11. A   12. D
13. C   14. A   15. B

CHAPTER 6 – Christ Works Miracles
Test Book pages 35–37

Matching
1. E   2. D   3. B   4. C   5. A

Multiple Choice
1. D   2. D   3. B   4. C   5. A   6. D   7. C   8. D   9. A   10. B

CHAPTER 7 – Christ, the Friend of the Sick
Test Book pages 39–41

Matching
1. E   2. C   3. A   4. B   5. D

Multiple Choice
1. D   2. C   3. A   4. A   5. C   6. A   7. D   8. A   9. C   10. D

CHAPTER 8 – Christ Casts Out Demons and Raises the Dead
Test Book pages 43–45

Matching
1. D   2. I   3. G   4. E   5. F   6. H   7. A   8. C   9. J   10. B

Multiple Choice
1. C   2. D   3. C   4. B   5. D   6. A   7. A   8. D   9. C   10. C

CHAPTER 9 – Christ, the Friend of the Poor
Test Book pages 47–49

Multiple Choice
1. D   2. C   3. A   4. D   5. C   6. B   7. C   8. A   9. B   10. D

CHAPTER 10 – Christ Founds His Church
Test Book pages 51–54

Multiple Choice
1. C   2. A   3. B   4. B   5. D   6. D   7. B   8. A   9. A   10. B   11. D   12. B
13. D   14. C   15. A   16. D   17. D   18. C   19. B   20. D

CHAPTER 11 – The Disciples Struggle to Understand
Test Book pages 55–57

Matching
1. E   2. E   3. E   4. B   5. C   6. D   7. A   8. C   9. D   10. D

Multiple Choice
1. C   2. C   3. D   4. A   5. B   6. D   7. A   8. D

PART THREE – How Christ Redeemed the World and Returned to Heaven

CHAPTER 12 – The Enemies of Christ
Test Book pages 59–63

Matching
1. D   2. C   3. A   4. E   5. B

Multiple Choice
1. A   2. B   3. C   4. B   5. A   6. D   7. A   8. C   9. B   10. C   11. A   12. B
13. D   14. C   15. C   16. D   17. A   18. C   19. A   20. D

CHAPTER 13 – The Last Days of Christ's Ministry
Test Book pages 65-67

Matching
1. B   2. G   3. H   4. G   5. A   6. F   7. C   8. I   9. E   10. D

Multiple Choice
1. B   2. D   3. B   4. A   5. B   6. D   7. A   8. B   9. C   10. D

CHAPTER 14 – Christ at the Last Supper and in the Garden
Test Book pages 69-71

Matching
1. C   2. F   3. G   4. A   5. B   6. E   7. D   8. A   9. H   10. A

Multiple Choice
1. C   2. C   3. A   4. B   5. D   6. B   7. C   8. D   9. A   10. C

CHAPTER 15 – Christ Before His Accusers
Test Book pages 73-75

Matching
1. C   2. D   3. E   4. F   5. A   6. B   7. E   8. I   9. H   10. G

Multiple Choice
1. D   2. A   3. C   4. B   5. A   6. D   7. D   8. C   9. D   10. C

CHAPTER 16 – Christ Is Crucified, Dies, and Is Buried
Test Book pages 77-79

Matching
1. G   2. I   3. D   4. H   5. J   6. E   7. A   8. C   9. F   10. B

Multiple Choice
1. B   2. D   3. B   4. A   5. A   6. C   7. C   8. D   9. B   10. A

CHAPTER 17 – The Proof of Christ's Divinity
Test Book pages 81-83

Matching
1. D   2. J   3. E   4. H   5. B   6. A   7. I   8. C   9. F   10. G

Multiple Choice
1. D   2. C   3. A   4. B   5. C   6. D   7. A   8. B   9. D   10. C

PART FOUR – How the Apostles Became the Foundation of the Church

CHAPTER 18 – The Growth of the Early Church
Test Book pages 85-87

Matching
1. H   2. G   3. F   4. A   5. B   6. E   7. B   8. B   9. D   10. C

Multiple Choice
1. D   2. B   3. D   4. C   5. A   6. B   7. A   8. C   9. A   10. B

CHAPTER 19 – The Seed of God Is Scattered
Test Book pages 89-91

Matching
1. F   2. C   3. D   4. J   5. A   6. J   7. C   8. E   9. B   10. D   11. H   12. I
13. G   14. I   15. A

Multiple Choice
1. D   2. C   3. C   4. A   5. B   6. C   7. D   8. B   9. C   10. B   11. A

CHAPTER 20 – Paul's Conversion and Early Ministry
Test Book pages 93-95

Matching
1. D   2. H   3. C   4. G   5. F   6. B   7. A   8. B   9. E   10. B

Multiple Choice
1. B   2. D   3. D   4. A   5. B   6. D   7. C   8. C   9. D   10. B

CHAPTER 21 – Paul Takes the Gospel to Europe
Test Book pages 97-99

Matching
1. D   2. H   3. J   4. B   5. F   6. A   7. E   8. I   9. C   10. G

Multiple Choice
1. B   2. A   3. D   4. D   5. A   6. C   7. A   8. C   9. B   10. D

CHAPTER 22 – Paul's Last Missionary Journey
Test Book pages 101-3

Matching
1. B   2. E   3. D   4. A   5. C

Multiple Choice
1. C   2. C   3. B   4. D   5. B   6. C   7. B   8. A   9. C   10. C

CHAPTER 23 – Paul in Jerusalem and Rome
Test Book pages 105-7

Matching
1. G   2. H   3. J   4. F   5. I   6. A   7. B   8. C   9. E   10. D

Multiple Choice
1. C   2. B   3. D   4. A   5. A   6. B   7. D   8. A   9. D   10. D

 TAN·BOOKS

TAN Books was founded in 1967 to preserve the spiritual, intellectual and liturgical traditions of the Catholic Church. At a critical moment in history TAN kept alive the great classics of the Faith and drew many to the Church. In 2008 TAN was acquired by Saint Benedict Press. Today TAN continues its mission to a new generation of readers.

From its earliest days TAN has published a range of booklets that teach and defend the Faith. Through partnerships with organizations, apostolates, and mission-minded individuals, well over 10 million TAN booklets have been distributed.

More recently, TAN has expanded its publishing with the launch of Catholic calendars and daily planners—as well as Bibles, fiction, and multimedia products through its sister imprints Catholic Courses (CatholicCourses.com) and Saint Benedict Press (SaintBenedictPress.com). In 2015, TAN Homeschool became the latest addition to the TAN family, preserving the Faith for the next generation of Catholics (www.TANHomeschool.com).

Today TAN publishes over 500 titles in the areas of theology, prayer, devotions, doctrine, Church history, and the lives of the saints. TAN books are published in multiple languages and found throughout the world in schools, parishes, bookstores and homes.

For a free catalog, visit us online at
TANBooks.com

Or call us toll-free at
(800) 437-5876